QUEST FOR ANSWERS

A Primer of Understanding and Treating Severe Personality Disorders

Salman Akhtar, M.D.

JASON ARONSON INC.
Northvale, New Jersey
London

Production Editor: Ruth E. Brody

This book was set in 11 point Times Roman by TechType of Upper Saddle River, New Jersey, and printed by Haddon Craftsmen in Scranton, Pennsylvania.

Library of Congress Cataloging-in-Publication Data

Akhtar, Salman, 1946 July 31–
    Quest for answers : a primer of understanding and treating severe
personality disorders / Salman Akhtar.
      p. cm.
    Includes bibliographical references and index.
    ISBN 1-56821-364-6
    1. Personality disorders — Miscellanea. I. Title.
RC554.A244 1994
616.85′8 — dc20
                                      94-22794

Manufactured in the United States of America. Jason Aronson Inc. offers books and cassettes. For information and catalog write to Jason Aronson Inc., 230 Livingston Street, Northvale, New Jersey 07647.

To
Irfan Salim
Naresh Julka
J. Anderson Thomson, Jr.
Julian Stern
and
Shantanu Maitra

Contents

PART II: STRUCTURE AND DYNAMICS

PART IV: EVALUATION AND TRIAGE

Preface

There is often a conflict between the student's legitimate demand for simplicity and the teacher's equally understandable dread of oversimplification. This book seeks to resolve such conflict in one particular area of clinical psychiatry. I am deeply thankful to my publisher, Jason Aronson, for suggesting its challenging format, my department chairman, Dr. Troy Thompson for creating an intellectual ambience conducive to such work, my patients for providing the basis for it, my family for the necessary emotional "holding environment," my students for asking good questions, and my secretary, Maryann Nevin, for skillful and pleasant assistance in preparing the manuscript. The wisdom of many teachers, the inspired counsel of many senior colleagues, and the lively input of many peers contribute to the positions I have taken in this book. I have thanked these distinguished individuals by name in my last book, *Broken Structures* (1992). Here I wish to avoid what Norman Kiell has called "the sin of repetition."

Part I

DIAGNOSIS AND DIFFERENTIAL DIAGNOSIS

1. What are the various severe personality disorders and what are their common characteristics?

There are eight types of severe personality disorders: narcissistic, borderline, schizoid, paranoid, hypomanic, antisocial, histrionic, and schizotypal. While different from each other in many respects, these disorders do have many similarities in their phenomenology, dynamics, psychostructural organization, and developmental background.

Descriptively, the individuals suffering from these disorders exhibit chronic restlessness, unstable emotions, vacillating relationships, unrealistic and contradictory life goals, excessive self-absorption, defective empathy, somewhat egocentric perception of reality, impaired capacity for mourning, inability to love, sexual difficulties, and moral defects of varying degrees. *Dynamically*, splitting or active dissociation of mutually contradictory self- and object representations is a major defensive operation in these conditions. This is accompanied by the subsidiary mechanisms of denial, primitive idealization, and projective identification. *Psychostructurally*, at this level of character organization there is a restriction of the conflict-free ego, poor superego internalization and integration, blurring of the ego-superego delimitation, and, most important, the lack of an integrated self-concept, resulting in the syndrome of identity diffusion. *Developmentally*, while variations in the degree of constitutional predisposition as well as in the nuance, timing, and intensity of childhood traumata and their psychic elaboration do exist, by and large these conditions are associated with an aborted separation-individuation process and the consequent failure to master the Oedipus complex. There is lack of object constancy, impaired capacity to maintain optimal distance, persistent infantile omnipotence, and much unneutralized aggression, with a tendency toward inhibited, perverse, or promiscuous sexuality.

3

Each severe personality disorder involves overt and covert characteristics in six areas of psychosocial functioning: self-concept; interpersonal relations; social adaptation; ethics, standards, and ideals; love and sexuality; and cognitive style. Overt and covert designations in this context do not necessarily imply conscious or unconscious existence, although such topographical distribution might also exist. In general, the overt and covert designations denote contradictory phenomenological aspects that are more or less discernible. The overt and covert clinical features are more rigidly separated in narcissistic, schizoid, hypomanic, and paranoid personalities than in borderline, antisocial, and histrionic personalities. In the latter three personality disorders, these sets of features often fluidly alternate in becoming surface phenomena. Even when there is a rigid separation between overt and covert features, the therapist's awareness of these individuals' inherently dichotomous selves encourages further inquiry and prevents misdiagnosis.

This manner of organizing the symptomatology of severe personality disorders emphasizes the centrality of splitting and identity diffusion in these conditions. It also presents a modern, dimensional system of personality diagnosis while retaining the traditional, categorical system of nosology.

SUGGESTED READINGS

Akhtar, S. (1992). *Broken Structures: Severe Personality Disorders and Their Treatment*, pp. 367-375. Northvale, NJ: Jason Aronson.

Kernberg, O. F. (1970). A psychoanalytic classification of character pathology. *Journal of the American Psychoanalytic Association* 18:800-822.

Mahler, M. S. and Kaplan, L. (1977). Developmental aspects in the assessment of narcissistic and so-called borderline personalities. In *Borderline Personality Disorders: The Concept, The Syndrome, The Patient*, ed. P. Hartocollis, pp. 71-86. New York: International Universities Press.

2. What are the clinical features of narcissistic personality disorder?

The cardinal feature of narcissistic personality disorder is heightened narcissism. Individuals with this disorder display grandiosity, intense ambition, and an insatiable craving for admiration. Their consuming self-interest renders them incapable of appreciating and understanding the independent motivations and needs of others. Consequently, they come across as cold, unempathic, exploitative, and unconcerned about those around them.

Narcissistic individuals have a grandiose *self-concept*. They give an appearance of self-sufficiency and are preoccupied with achieving outstanding success. Covertly, however, they are fragile, vulnerable to shame, sensitive to criticism, and filled with morose self-doubts and feelings of inferiority.

Their *interpersonal relations* are extensive but exploitative and driven by an intense need for tribute from others. They are unable to participate genuinely in group activities and, in family life, value children over the spouse. Inwardly, they are deeply envious of others' capacity for meaningful engagement with life. They attempt to hide such envy by scorn for others; this may, in turn, be masked by pseudohumility.

Capable of consistent hard work, narcissistic individuals often achieve professional success and high levels of *social adaptation*. However, they are preoccupied with appearances and their work is done mainly to seek admiration (pseudosublimation). The overly zealous vocational commitment masks a dilettante-like attitude, chronic boredom, and gnawing aimlessness.

Their *ethics, standards, and ideals* display an apparent enthusiasm for sociopolitical affairs, a caricatured modesty, and pretended contempt for money in real life. At the same time, they are often quite materialistic, ready to shift values to gain favor, irreverent toward authority, and prone to pathologic lying and cutting ethical corners.

A similar contradiction is evident in the realm of *love and sexuality*. Overtly, narcissistic individuals are charming, seductive, and given to extramarital affairs, even promiscuity. Covertly, however, they draw little gratification beyond physical pleasure from sexuality and are unable to have deep and sustained romantic relations. Moreover, they seem unable to genuinely accept the incest taboo and are vulnerable to sexual perversions.

Superficially, their *cognitive style* suggests a decisive, opinionated, and strikingly supple intellect. However, their knowledge is often limited to trivia ("headline intelligence") and they are forgetful of details. Their capacity for learning is also compromised since learning forces one to acknowledge one's ignorance and they find this unacceptable. They are articulate but tend to use language and speaking for regulating self-esteem rather than communicating.

In short, narcissistic personality disorder is characterized by a defensively inflated self-concept fueled by fantasies of glory, protected by being constantly admired for social success, and buttressed by scornful devaluation of those who stir up envy. Underneath this grandiose self-concept (not infrequently built around some real talent or special aptitude) lie disturbing feelings of inferiority, self-doubt, boredom, alienation, and aimlessness.

SUGGESTED READINGS

Akhtar, S. (1989). Narcissistic personality disorder. *Psychiatric Clinics of North America* 12:505–529.

Freud, S. (1914). On narcissism: an introduction. *Standard Edition* 14:67–103.

Kernberg, O. F. (1975). *Borderline Conditions and Pathological Narcissism*, pp. 227–314. New York: Jason Aronson.

3. What are the clinical features of borderline personality disorder?

The main clinical features of borderline personality disorder include unstable identity, affective instability, and intense interpersonal relationships that vacillate between extremes of idealization and devaluation. Individuals with borderline personality disorder constantly fluctuate between murderous rage and suicidal despair on the one hand and worshiping awe and smug exaltation on the other hand. They are action-prone, impulsive and self-destructive. Most importantly, they lack a coherent sense of self. Their *self-concept* is unstable and oscillates between feelings of hapless inferiority and condescending superiority. Mostly, they feel defective, "bad," and victimized. However, they lack humility and have a core of omnipotence, conceit, and self-righteousness. They have unclear and contradictory life goals, fragile gender identity, and vulnerability to dreadful feelings of emptiness.

Their *interpersonal relations* are intense. They cling to others and seem quite dependent. At the same time, they do not truly comprehend the separate existence and independent motivations of others. As a result, their relationships are based upon need satisfaction and are essentially exploitative. They fluctuate not only between idealization and devaluation of others but also between extremes of closeness and distance from them.

Superficially, they may have an adequate *social adaptation*. However, a closer look at their life reveals an erratic academic and/or vocational record and often much geographical mobility over time.

In the realm of *love and sexuality* too, borderline individuals show contradictions. They are vulnerable to frequent, intense infatuations and often are sexually promiscuous. However, they easily fall out of love and their sexual interest wanes in monogamous relationships. They also have a tendency toward perversions and an incapacity for deep and sustained romantic relations.

Their *ethics, standards, and ideals* are also riddled with contradictions. They show much enthusiasm about moral and ethical matters but are readily corruptible. They often succumb to charismatic preachers and esoteric cults. Their capacity to experience genuine guilt is weak and their inner restraints on behavior center around shame, fear, and a paranoid dread of exposure.

Their *cognitive style* is characterized by a reckless decisiveness that is often readily regretted and reversed. They tend to see things in black and white terms. In unstructured situations, they lapse into primary process thinking. When well directed and coexistent with inherent talent, this tendency may yield significant artistic and poetic creativity. Out of control, it contributes to such individuals' vulnerability to brief and reversible psychotic breaks.

In sum, borderline personality disorder is characterized by a pervasive instability of mood, vacillating interpersonal relations, ill-formed identity, and a brittle cognitive organization. There is a contradictory presence of intense affects with a dreadful sense of inner emptiness. In addition, there is intolerance of being alone, leading to compulsive socialization and yet a tendency to abruptly withdraw from people for short periods of time. An inordinate sensitivity to rejection, a chaotic sexual life, a propensity towards substance abuse, and marked impulsivity, often with self-destructive results, complete the clinical picture.

SUGGESTED READINGS

Gunderson, J. G., and Singer, M. (1975). Defining borderline patients: an overview. *American Journal of Psychiatry* 133:1–10.

Kernberg, O. F. (1967). Borderline personality organization. *Journal of the American Psychoanalytic Association* 15:641–685.

Stone, M. H. (1980). *The Borderline Syndrome*, pp. 5–33. New York: McGraw-Hill.

4. What are the clinical features of schizoid personality disorder?

The chief clinical feature of schizoid personality disorder is social withdrawal, which is a vehement defense against a threateningly intense need for object relations. Individuals with schizoid personality disorder appear cold, aloof, and uninterested in others. Inwardly, however, they are highly attuned to others and desirous of personal contact and intimacy.

On the surface, their *self-concept* is stoic, non-competitive, compliant, and markedly self-sufficient. Covertly, however, they are exquisitely sensitive and in need of love, a fact that is missed in the DSM-IV description of schizoid personality emphasizing only the impervious exterior.

Schizoid individuals have limited *interpersonal relations*. They appear withdrawn, insensitive to other people's emotions, and afraid of intimacy. Underneath this detached persona lie intense curiosity about others, a need to connect with them, and a sense of guilt over lacking feelings for others. When separated from important others, schizoid individuals feel utterly insecure and lost but when reunited with them, they fear being swallowed, smothered, and absorbed. As a result, they show subtle oscillations in their distance from others.

Their *social adaptation* varies. In general, they prefer solitary occupational and recreational activities. However, with carefully selected intimates, they can be quite lively (in Bleuler's terms, "enlarged autism among people of same persuasion"). They seem lazy but are capable of passionate endurance in the selected spheres of their own interests. In the context of abstract ideas especially, schizoid individuals can make quite creative and original contributions.

In the realm of *love and sexuality*, their life is superficially quite restricted. They seem free of romantic interests and are averse to sexual innuendo and gossip. Secretly, they often have voyeuristic and pornographic interests and are vulnerable to compulsive masturbation.

Their *ethics, standards, and ideals* are often idiosyncratic, with a leaning toward the mystical and the parapsychological. At the same time, they show a peculiar moral unevenness, being highly self-sacrificing one moment and strikingly amoral the next. Their *cognitive style* is characterized by vagueness, absentmindedness, and odd fluctuations between clumsy inarticulateness and nimble eloquence. Despite their appearance to the contrary, they are quite observant and highly attuned to their environment. They have a rich inner fantasy life and are hyper-reflective about themselves.

In essence, schizoid personality disorder is overtly characterized by social withdrawal, interpersonal detachment, solitariness in vocational and recreational choices, asexuality, idiosyncratic morality, and absentmindedness. Covertly, however, the schizoid individual is exquisitely sensitive, emotionally needy, acutely observant, creative, often perverse, and vulnerable to corruption. The avoidance of and the need for others, the callous persona and the inner sensitivity, and the absent-mindedness and vigilance are various facets of the same condition. The tension between these extremes is the heart of the schizoid pathology.

SUGGESTED READINGS

Akhtar, S. (1987). Schizoid personality disorder: a synthesis of developmental, dynamic, and descriptive features. *American Journal of Psychotherapy* 41:499–518.

Fairbairn, W. R. D. (1940). Schizoid factors in the personality. In *An Object Relations Theory of the Personality*, pp. 3–27. New York: Basic Books.

Guntrip, H. (1969). The schizoid personality and the external world. In *Schizoid Phenomena, Object Relations and the Self*, pp. 17–48. New York: International Universities Press.

5. What are the clinical features of paranoid personality disorder?

The main clinical feature of paranoid personality disorder is a pervasive mistrust of others. Individuals with paranoid personality are highly suspicious, feel unjustly treated by others, and regard themselves as the object of hostility, interference, and oppression. They are chronically irritable and behave in a boastful, impatient, and obstinate manner. They constantly complain, seek justice, and are frequently litigious.

Paranoid individuals have a hidden core of timidity, fear, and inferiority against which they extract an over-confident, intimidating, unduly formal, and grandiose *self-concept*. Scornful and contemptuous of others, they can easily become enraged. Covertly, though, they are doubt-ridden and guilty over their aggression toward others.

Their *interpersonal relations* are characterized by mistrust, aloofness, and emotional detachment. They lack a sense of humor and are uncomfortable with physical intimacy. They also have a habitual pattern of holding grudges and seeking revenge. At the same time, they can be strikingly naïve and gullible, with a special vulnerability to belief in gossip.

Their *social adaptation* is characterized by an industrious and driven attitude that may lead to success in solitary, critical lines of work. However, they have repeated interpersonal difficulties, few friends at the workplace, and little capacity to enjoy "softer" things such as music, poetry, fiction, and so forth.

Paranoid individuals show much discomfort in the realm of *love and sexuality*. On the surface, they seem to be devoid of romantic interests and averse to sexual innuendo or gossip. Underneath this dry persona, they carry a vulnerability to erotomania, an undue sensitivity to pregenital trends in others, latent homosexuality, and a tendency toward sadomasochistic perversions.

Their *ethics, standards, and ideals* display a literal, rule-bound, moralistic stance on the one hand and an expedient mendacity, crafty manipulativeness, and subtle sociopathic tendencies on the other. They value intellectual prowess and are prone to ethnic and religious fanaticism.

The *cognitive style* of individuals with paranoid personality disorder deserves special mention. Overtly, they have a legalistic bent, sharp attention, rich vocabulary, hypervigilance, and a tendency toward perceptual hairsplitting; they often possess striking oratorial skills. Covertly, however, they are unable to grasp the "big picture." They readily dismiss the obvious, including any evidence that is contradictory to their preexisting beliefs. Their attention is narrow and biased. They are experts in seeing the "truth" but almost always fail to grasp the "whole truth."

In sum, individuals with paranoid personality disorder are overtly arrogant, mistrustful, driven, and often successful in solitary professions, moralistic, and sharply vigilant toward the external environment. However, covertly, they are timid, gullible, corruptible, vulnerable to erotomania and sadomasochistic perversions, and cognitively unable to grasp the totality of actual events in their proper context.

SUGGESTED READINGS

Akhtar, S. (1990). Paranoid personality disorder: a synthesis of developmental, dynamic, and descriptive features. *American Journal of Psychotherapy* 44:5–25.

Blum, H. P. (1981). Object inconstancy and paranoid conspiracy. *Journal of the American Psychoanalytic Association* 29:789–813.

Kraepelin, E. (1921). *Manic Depressive Illness and Paranoia*, pp. 268–272. Edinburgh, Scotland: E. S. Livingstone.

6. What are the clinical features of antisocial personality disorder?

The cardinal feature of antisocial personality disorder is an incapacity for experiencing genuine inner guilt and the associated lack of concern for others. Individuals with antisocial personality display a predominantly narcissistic orientation in which even the seeming islands of devotion hide selfish motives. They have an excessive sensitivity to displeasure, an "addiction to novelty," and a highly cynical view of the world.

Their *self-concept* is that of a victim and an exception to ordinary social rules. They fluctuate between spells of infantile helplessness and self-inflated omnipotence. On the one hand, they are self-centered and exhibitionistic, and on the other, they suffer from feelings of inferiority and emptiness.

A superficial affability covers up their basic tendency to be disaffiliated in *interpersonal relations*. They are quick in reading people for manipulative purposes and can develop rapid intimacy with others. At the same time, they mistrust everyone and lack empathy with the enduring aspects of others' characters. They lack an inner appreciation of generational boundaries and have an impaired capacity for respect.

Their *social adaptation*, when seen in a brief cross-section of time, reveals a playful and thrill-seeking individual who seems earnestly interested in the vocational opportunities offered by life though is somewhat over-ambitious and preoccupied with appearances. A longitudinal account of their lives, however, reveals poor academic records, checkered vocational histories, the use of aliases, a chronic search for shortcuts to money, and the existence of hidden lives.

In the realm of *love and sexuality*, antisocial individuals are manipulative, promiscuous, unable to love, and incapable of viewing the romantic partner as a separate individual with his/her own interests, rights, and values. They also have difficulty in genuinely comprehending the incest taboo and show a proclivity for perversions.

It is, however, in the area of *ethics, standards, and ideals* that their pathology is most marked. They show a profound lack of guilt and a consistent disregard for law and social mores. Such severe superego pathology manifests not only in an incapacity for self-reflective sadness but also in lying, swindling, forgery, prostitution, and, at times, even assault, robbery, and murder.

Their *cognitive style* is characterized by a superficial glibness with a smattering of art, literature, and technical jargon in conversation. However, their knowledge is limited to trivia ("headline intelligence") and their ideas lack originality. Quick to learn delinquent skills, they show a peculiar inability to learn the ordinary and the expected.

In sum, antisocial personality disorder is characterized by overt grandiosity, affability, earnestness, seductiveness, and articulateness. Covertly, however, individuals with antisocial personality are inferiority laden, scornful of others, incapable of love, profoundly lacking in the capacity for guilt and remorse, and possessing only exhibitionistic tidbits of knowledge. Active or passive criminal tendencies often accompany the condition, but since criminality is not a psychological concept these should not form the basis for the diagnosis.

SUGGESTED READINGS

Eissler, K. R., ed. (1949). *Searchlights on Delinquency: Essays in Honor of August Aichhorn*. New York: International Universities Press.

Johnson, A. M., and Szurek, S. A. (1952). The genesis of antisocial acting out in children and adults. *Psychoanalytic Quarterly* 21:323–343.

Kernberg, O. F. (1989). The narcissistic personality disorder and the differential diagnosis of antisocial behavior. *Psychiatric Clinics of North America* 12:553–570.

7. What is schizotypal personality disorder?

Schizotypal personality disorder is a relatively new diagnostic entity. It was introduced by *DSM-III* into psychiatric nosology. The term *schizotypal* is derived from a condensation of the two words, (*schizophrenia* and *genotype*) The idea behind delineating such a syndrome had its origins in two traditions. The first of these emanated from observations of behavioral peculiarities in nonpsychotic relatives of schizophrenics. The second grew out of the observation that some patients had all the core symptoms of schizophrenia but were not manifestly psychotic.

These clinical observations received theoretical underpinnings from Rado's and Meehl's hypotheses regarding a "schizotypal" disorder and the later genetic studies of schizophrenia. Rado hypothesized that the schizotypal individuals had essentially the same two constitutional defects that underlay schizophrenia: a deficiency in integrating pleasurable experiences and a distorted awareness of the bodily self. Their manifest symptoms emanated from these two defects. Basically, these symptoms were (1) chronic √ anhedonia and poor development of pleasurable emotions such as love, pride, joy, enthusiasm, and affection, (2) continual engulf-√ ment in emergency emotions such as fear and rage, (3) hypersensitivity to rejection, (4) feelings of alienation from everything and everyone, (5) rudimentary sexual life, and (6) propensity for(cognitive disorganization under stress.

Post-*DSM-III* studies supported the existence of such a syndrome. At the same time, it was found that social isolation, inadequate rapport, odd communication, and suspiciousness were more discriminating features of the condition and cognitive-perceptual disturbances were not as salient. *DSM-III-R*, therefore, presented a slightly revised picture of the disorder. It portrayed schizotypal personality disorder as a pervasive pattern of deficits in interpersonal relatedness and peculiarities of ideation, appearance, and behavior as manifested by at least five of the following:)

(1) ideas of reference, (2) undue social anxiety, (3) magical thinking, (4) unusual perceptual experiences, (5) odd or eccentric behavior or appearance, (6) no close friends, (7) odd speech, and (8) inappropriate affect.

Insofar as the introduction of schizotypal personality disorder illuminates the understudied overlap between psychoses and character pathology, it is a nosologically advanced step and is therefore welcome. However, such conceptualization does lead to two difficulties. First, in what appears to be a historically regressive step, it causes an artificial restriction of the definition of schizophrenia to only its floridly psychotic phases and forms. Second, it is logically inconsistent for the current psychiatric nosology to include a schizophrenic-spectrum disorder in the personality disorder section while excluding affective-spectrum disorders from it. Either the spectrum disorders of both types should be classified with their parent disorders on Axis I or both should be listed under personality disorders. My preference is for the latter alternative since it discourages the artificial separation of character pathology and major psychoses, and since it aligns us with our classic literature, which astutely recognized many personality disorders as "fundamental states" of psychotic disorders.

SUGGESTED READINGS

Diagnostic and Statistical Manual of Mental Disorders (1987). 3rd ed. revised, pp. 340–342. Washington, DC: American Psychiatric Association.

Meehl, P. E. (1962). Schizotaxia, schizotypy, schizophrenia. *American Psychologist* 17:827–838.

Rado, S. (1953). Dynamics and classification of disordered behavior. *American Journal of Psychiatry* 110:406–410.

8. What are the similarities and differences between borderline and narcissistic personalities?

The main similarity between borderline and narcissistic personalities pertains to their defensive organization. Both conditions are characterized by a marked use of the mechanism of splitting as reflected in the presence, in their inner worlds, of mutually dissociated or split-off self- and object representations. Thus, feelings of grandiosity, uniqueness, and supreme lovability coexist in them with equally convincing feelings of profound inferiority, inner badness, and unlovability. These splitting mechanisms are buttressed by primitive idealization, projective identification, omnipotent control, devaluation, and narcissistic withdrawal. Developmentally, both borderline and narcissistic individuals give evidence of an aborted separation-individuation process, lack of object constancy, and a distorted and incompletely mastered Oedipus complex. In both conditions, there is a pathological condensation of genital and pregenital conflicts under the overriding influence of pregenital, especially oral, aggression. Phenomenologically, both display troubled interpersonal relationships, chronic restlessness, excessive self-absorption, defective empathy, inability to love, and subtle defects of morality.

Borderline and narcissistic personalities, however, also differ in important ways. In borderline personality disorder, the self is poorly integrated and at chronic risk of dissolution into psychoticlike states; interpersonal stress or psychoactive substances frequently unmask this vulnerability. In narcissistic personality, however, the self, despite being unrealistically inflated (the "grandiose self"), is more cohesive and less in danger of regressive fragmentation. The borderline individual feels inferior to everybody else, but his frequently conceited attitude demonstrates grandiosity. The narcissistic patient, in contrast, is overtly self-assured and grandiose, only to be privately shame laden, hungry, and insecure. Identity diffusion is more overt in borderline disorder than in narcissistic disorder, where an enthusiastic, yet shallow, vocational commitment hides the inner aimlessness. Because of their greater cohesion, narcissistic personalities show better occupational function, greater tolerance for aloneness, and better impulse control than borderline personalities. Self-mutilation and persistent rage, frequent in borderline personality, are not associated with narcissistic personality. The narcissist shows a sharpened reasoning when angry, whereas the borderline, when enraged, becomes flustered, illogical, and chaotically explosive.

The developmental background of the two is also different. With narcissistic patients, one usually finds that as children, they were treated by their parents in an unempathic, cold, even spiteful, but nonetheless special, manner. This is perhaps because many of them were either first-born or only children, possessed special attributes (e.g., talent, outstanding intelligence, or physical charm), or occupied a particularly meaningful place in the mythic history of the family. Borderline individuals, in contrast, frequently come from families broken due to parental death or divorce. As children, they suffered from extreme frustrations, traumatic ruptures of the caretaking environment, and even physical and sexual abuse.

SUGGESTED READINGS

Adler, G. (1981). The borderline-narcissistic personality disorders continuum. *American Journal of Psychiatry* 138:46–50.

Kernberg, O. F. (1975). *Borderline Conditions and Pathological Narcissism*, pp. 264–270. New York: Jason Aronson.

Volkan, V. D. (1982). Narcissistic personality disorder. In *Critical Problems in Psychiatry*, ed. J. O. Cavenar and H. K. H. Brodie, pp. 332–350. Philadelphia, PA: Lippincott.

9. Are hysterical and histrionic personalities the same?

No. Histrionic personality disorder is distinct from hysterical personality disorder. Individuals with hysterical personality disorder (a diagnosis unfortunately not included in *DSM-IV*), though affectualized and unwittingly seductive, possess an intact identity, a capacity for stable, discriminating, and empathic interpersonal relationships, and a predominance of defense mechanisms centering on repression. Individuals with histrionic personality disorder, in contrast, show identity diffusion, predominance of splitting over repression, inability to integrate the contradictory aspects of self and others, marked superego defects, and restriction of autonomous ego functions.

Hysterical individuals have a neurotic personality organization and histrionic individuals a borderline personality organization. Hysterical individuals are suggestible only within the context of sexually embroidered and idealized triangular relationships. Histrionic individuals are, however, sexually less inhibited and may indeed be quite promiscuous; they are also vulnerable to substance abuse and addictions. Hysterical individuals show a clear distinction of attitudes toward the two sexes with much competitiveness with the same sex. Histrionic individuals show less differentiation in behavior toward men and women and are less competitive in general.

Hysterical individuals come from intact, strongly bonded families. Histrionic individuals come from disturbed, often broken families where adequate maternal care was unavailable to them. Hysterical individuals give a history of steady educational and vocational careers, and are capable of maintaining long-term relationships. Histrionic individuals have erratic academic and vocational careers and seem unable to maintain friendships over time.

To be sure, there are similarities between the two types. Both are dramatic, attention seeking, talkative, and affectualized.

However, each characteristic of the hysteric appears in exaggerated form in the histrionic which corresponds to what was earlier termed infantile, hysteroid, hysteriform borderline, oral hysteric, and sick hysteric personalities. Overtly, the individuals with histrionic personality are compliant and ingratiating, lively and friendly, readily interested in social and vocational opportunities, crudely and desperately seductive, enthusiastic about moral and ethical issues, and cognitively quick and decisive. However, covertly they are ridden with feelings of "badness" and inferiority, highly dependent yet narcissistically manipulative, corruptible, promiscuous, impulsive, vulnerable to addictions, vocationally erratic, and cognitively inattentive to details.

Histrionic individuals need to be distinguished from borderline individuals as well. Like the latter, they are clinging, needy, manipulative, impulsive, corruptible, and vulnerable to promiscuity and substance abuse. However, unlike borderlines, histrionic individuals do not display chronic rage and self-destructiveness. They are interpersonally more amiable and overtly less disturbed.

SUGGESTED READINGS

Cooper, A. M. (1987). Histrionic, narcissistic, and compulsive personality disorders. In *Diagnosis and Clarification in Psychiatry: A Critical Appraisal of* DSM-III, ed. G. Tischler, pp. 290–299. New York: Columbia University Press.

Kernberg, O. F. (1985). Hysterical and histrionic personality disorders. In *Psychiatry*, vol. 1, ed. R. Michels and J. O. Cavenar, pp. 1–12. Philadelphia, PA: Lippincott.

Zetzel, E. (1968). The so-called good hysteric. *International Journal of Psycho-Analysis* 49:256–260.

10. Is there such an entity as hypomanic personality disorder?

Yes. Classics in descriptive psychiatry including the writings of Ziehen, Kraepelin, Bleuler, Kretschmer, Jaspers, and Schneider have consistently maintained that there exists such a disorder as hypomanic personality. British psychiatric textbooks, too, recognize the disorder and the *International Classification of Diseases* (9th revision, 1980) includes *chronic hypomanic personality disorder* as a distinct and separate nosological entity. However, the disorder has not yet found its way into the official psychiatric nomenclature in the United States, where the character pathology related to affective disorders is listed along with the pertinent Axis I or state disorders. This is not to say that hypomanic personality disorder has gone completely unrecognized here. Indeed, contemporary American investigators within both descriptive psychiatry (e.g., Winokur, Akiskal) and psychoanalysis (e.g., Kernberg, Volkan, Akhtar) have described this entity and many of them lament its exclusion from the current official nomenclature.

Individuals with hypomanic personality disorder, like those with other severe personality disorders, display characteristic overt and covert manifestations in six areas of psychosocial functioning. In the area of *self concept*, they appear grandiose, self-confident, robust, problem free, cheerful and unduly optimistic. However, they also have morose self-doubts and a profound difficulty with contemplative aloneness and sadness.

Their *interpersonal relations* are characterized by superficial idealization of others and rapid development of intimacy. However, they secretly have contempt for others and soon lose interest in people. Alongside such flightiness, they have intensely dependent relationships with one or two individuals.

In the realm of *social adaptation* they appear decisive, daring, energetic, and work addicted. Their self-assured entrepreneurial attitude often propels them into leadership roles where even their meddlesome tendencies are tolerated. They also tend to take too many risks and might display questionable judgment in social and financial matters.

Their behavior in the area of *love and sexuality* is characterized by flirtatiousness, fondness for sexual innuendo, extramarital liaisons, and promiscuity. They seem unable to be genuinely involved with a romantic partner viewed with equal regard and sustained emotional and sensual interests.

Their *ethics, standards, and ideals* show many contradictions. Overtly, they seem zealous about ethical and moral matters and proclaim fantastically high ideals for themselves and others. Covertly, they cut ethical corners, mock authority, and are quite corruptible.

Individuals with hypomanic personality disorder are glib, articulate, given to punning, and "hyper" on the surface. However, a deeper look at their *cognitive style* reveals superficiality of knowledge, subtle learning defects, and lack of systematic approach and objective outlook to their various plans.

In sum, the individual with a hypomanic personality is overtly cheerful, highly social, given to idealization of others, work addicted, flirtatious, and articulate. Covertly, the person is guilty over his aggression toward others, incapable of aloneness, defective in empathy, unable to love, corruptible, and lacking a systematic approach in his cognitive life style.

SUGGESTED READINGS

Akhtar, S. (1988). Hypomanic personality disorder. *Integrative Psychiatry* 6:37–52.

Akiskal, H. D. (1984). Characterologic manifestations of affective disorders: toward a new conceptualization. *Integrative Psychiatry* 2:83–88.

Kretschmer, E. (1925). *Physique and Character*, trans. W. J. H. Sprott, pp. 126–149. New York: Harcourt Brace.

11. What is meant by the "as-if" personality?

The term "as-if" personality was introduced into psychoanalytic and psychiatric literature by Helene Deutsch in 1942. Although the concept has been elaborated upon by later contributors, especially Greenacre, Ross, Katan, and, more recently, Gediman, its portrayal by Deutsch remains an unquestioned classic.

Deutsch (1942) applied this term to certain individuals suffering from a character disorder that "forces on the observer the inescapable impression that the individual's whole relationship to life has something about it which is lacking in genuineness and yet outwardly runs along 'as-if' it were complete" (p. 302). However, these individuals themselves do not seem aware of their defect in feeling. While a bit too verbally facile and dilettantish, they superficially seem well adjusted and might even display appropriate emotional responsiveness. Yet something subtle and intangible is missing, leading their friends and acquaintances to wonder what is wrong with them.

Deeper contact with "as-if" personalities reveals that they are almost totally devoid of object constancy. Consequently, they are unable to have empathy with enduring aspects of others' characters. They do, however, display a remarkable attunement to others' expectations, which helps them to adapt to their environment. They lack authenticity and display a tendency toward rapid narcissistic identifications with others. These identifications are not assimilated into the self-system but are acted out in a superficial manner. This tendency to mimic others has many purposes. It helps buttress their fragile and weak inner self. It also serves to deny any distance, difference, and disagreement with others and thus assures their continued support. Aggressive tendencies are split off, lending such individuals an air of "negative goodness" and of mild amiability. All this contributes to a corruptible value system and striking defects of morality. Ideologies and sociopolitical groups valued one day can readily be discarded in favor of different, even contradictory, affiliations if circumstances change.

"As-if" personalities almost invariably give a history of maternal deprivation and unstable, shifting, and multiple care-takers during the first few years of childhood. The basic trauma they have suffered is the failure to find sustained objects for emotional investment. The process of identification in them has not progressed beyond imitativeness. Their inner psychic structure is weak, and the superego (which requires a meaningful, deep oedipal experience) is grossly deficient.

The emotional incapacity of "as if" individuals is different from the apparent blandness of repressed individuals. In the latter, a highly differentiated emotional life is hidden behind a defensive wall. In "as-if" personalities, the loss of affect represents a real loss of inner object cathexes. The "as-if" personality should also be distinguished from the "pseudo as-if" personality in which the experience of inauthenticity is limited to specific life situations and skills and is consciously felt by the individual. The potential for affect is greater in such people. Their inauthenticity is based upon anxious retreat from genuineness and not upon structural deficits typical of the "as-if" personality.

SUGGESTED READINGS

Deutsch, H. (1942). Some forms of emotional disturbance and their relationship to schizophrenia. *Psychoanalytic Quarterly* 11:301–321.
Gediman, H. (1985). Imposture, inauthenticity and feeling fraudulent. *Journal of the American Psychoanalytic Association* 33:911–936.
Ross, N. (1967). The "as-if" personality. *Journal of the American Psychoanalytic Association* 15:59–82.

12. Are there sex-related differences in severe personality disorders?

Yes. Sex-related differences do seem to exist in the incidence and prevalence of severe personality disorders. Narcissistic, antisocial, schizoid, schizotypal, and paranoid personality disorders are more common in men, while histrionic and borderline personality disorders occur more often in women. The meaning of these differences, however, remains unclear. Many factors could account for them. For instance, diagnostic biases of clinicians might lead them to assign one label (e.g., narcissistic) more often to men and another (e.g., borderline) to women. Or, the different prevalence could result from a referral artifact. In other words, while equal numbers of men and women might have narcissistic personality disorder, for various reasons more men end up seeking psychiatric help for it and are therefore overrepresented in clinical samples. The sex-related differences in severe personality disorders, however, go beyond incidence and prevalence. The symptomatology of these disorders in the two sexes also seems to differ. Paranoid personality disorder, for example, has been described to occur in two forms; one passively resentful, quasi-masochistic, secretive, and cynically brooding, and the other arrogant, actively defiant, openly hostile, angry, and litigious. The former seems to have a kinship with schizoid personality and the latter with narcissistic personality. The various explanations for these differences include the hypothesis of the two types being sex-related epiphenomena. The silently resentful outcome is supposedly more frequent in women and the blatantly defiant more frequent in men.

A similar situation might exist in relation to antisocial personality disorder. A passive-parasitic pattern of it seems more common in women and an aggressive-criminal pattern more common in men. The situation might, however, be even more complex. It is possible that the disorder, reportedly three times more common in men, has been kept from becoming floridly manifest in women by the greater societal restraints upon them. With the advent of increased freedom for women, perhaps one will see more female antisocial characters. On the other hand, constitutional differences between the two sexes, especially those involving aggression and motor-mindedness (and their effects upon psychic development), could also determine this differential prevalence. Indeed, a common diagnosis for antisocial and histrionic personality disorders has been suggested, with the underlying disorder manifesting itself as antisocial in men and histrionic in women.

Finally, could the greater prevalence of narcissistic personality among men represent, besides diagnostic biases and referral artifacts, a genuine difference in the sex-related incidence of the disorder? In that case, could it be that the male psychosexual development, or perhaps even the gender-determined differences in the separation-individuation process of the two sexes, contribute to these differences? Clearly, these are provocative questions, but few definitive answers exist at this time. Two things, however, are clear. First, there do seem to be some sex-related differences in the prevalence and symptomatology of severe personality disorders. Second, this is an ill-understood and murky area that warrants further, sophisticated investigation.

SUGGESTED READINGS

Akhtar, S., Byrne, J. P., and Doghramji, K. (1986). The demographic profile of borderline personality disorder. *Journal of Clinical Psychiatry* 47:196–198.
Diagnostic and Statistical Manual of Mental Disorders (1987). 3rd ed. revised, pp. 335–358. Washington, DC: American Psychiatric Association.
Reich, J. (1987). Sex distribution of *DSM-III* personality disorders in psychiatric outpatients. *American Journal of Psychiatry* 144:485–488.

13. How does culture affect the prevalence and manifestations of these conditions?

Few reliable cross-cultural studies of severe personality disorders exist. However, from the data that is available it seems that *severe personality disorders are universal in their prevalence.* The frequency with which individuals with such disorders come to clinical attention might, however, vary with the levels of affluence, optimism, religiosity, psychological awareness, and medical orientation in the society. For instance, only one to three percent of psychiatric outpatients in Ethiopia and India have personality disorders while the corresponding figure for British outpatients is thirty-two percent. Variations in diagnostic practices and in the help-seeking patterns of the three societies are more likely to account for this striking finding than actual differences in incidence.

A particular culture might facilitate a specific phenotypal outcome of character pathology. Its modal child-rearing practices might be both the etiologic agents of intrapsychic conflicts and formal conduits to their ego-syntonic expressions, either way contributing eminently to the future character armor. Cultures where child rearing typically is suppressive of affects (especially those related to aggression) and discouraging of individuation favor schizoid and "as-if" phenotypal outcomes of severe character pathology. In contrast, cultures that allow freer discharge of affect and encourage assertion and individuation favor narcissistic, borderline, and paranoid phenomenologies. *Even within a particular form of severe personality disorder, actual symptomatology might be affected by culturally held value systems.* For instance, a grandiose asceticism ("moral narcissism") is a more frequent accompaniment of narcissistic personality disorder in the East and a materialistically acquisitive picture more common in the West. (This is not to espouse the overly sociological perspective that identity diffusion is a phenomenon specific to the twentieth century and narcissism to contemporary Western culture.) On a less deep level, easy access to alcohol, drugs, perverse sexual outlets, pornography, and firearms in Western (especially North American) society tends to render the overt manifestations of borderline, histrionic, and antisocial personalities dangerous and more flagrant. Less permissive societies yield more muted manifestations of these disorders. Japanese borderline patients, for instance, are less often drug and alcohol dependent than their American counterparts.

Even within a particular culture, subgroup differences exist. The lesser frequency with which the diagnosis of borderline personality disorder is used for blacks in this country is a case in point. Diagnostic biases, referral artifacts, and pathoplastic effects of culture, however, need to be ruled out before assuming that there is truly a lower incidence of the disorder among blacks.

Finally, cultural factors might also underlie those differences in the prevalence and manifestations of severe personality disorders that seem gender-related. For instance, the much lower prevalence of antisocial personality disorders among females might be related in part to the greater societal restraints on women's behavior. With shifting societal attitudes that are allowing women more freedom and greater access to all means of self-expression, the remarkable infrequency of antisocial personality among them might no longer remain so infrequent.

SUGGESTED READINGS

Green, A. (1986). Moral narcissism. In *On Private Madness*, pp. 115–141. New Haven, CT: International Universities Press.

Ikuta, N., Zanarini, M. C., Minakawa, K., et al. (1993). Axis I disorders of American and Japanese BPD patients. *CME Syllabus and Proceedings Summary: 146th Annual Meeting*. Washington, DC: American Psychiatric Association.

Khandelwal, S. K. and Workneh, F. (1988). Psychiatric outpatients in a general hospital of Ethiopia. *The International Journal of Social Psychiatry* 34:230–235.

14. Are the severe personality disorders always associated with low-level social functioning?

No. This is an impression derived exclusively from clinical samples. While severe character pathology does affect social functioning adversely, this is not necessarily the case. Many individuals with severe personality disorders never seek psychiatric help and function relatively well. Some of them even acquire social prominence and outstanding success. The fields in which they might do so, however, vary with the specific constellations of their character traits.

Narcissistic personalities, for instance, gravitate toward administrative positions of power and exhibitionistic vocations (e.g., the media and the entertainment business) that gratify their need to be looked up to and admired. They may become quite successful in these lines of work, and, upon acquiring power, may restructure their social reality by eliminating or controlling envied others. Moreover, the constant adulation they receive from others may amply compensate them for their inner despair. At the same time, it is true that a careful look at their productivity over a long period of time often reveals a certain lack of depth and flightiness in their work. *"As-if"* *personalities* might find in stage or screen acting and professional mimicry a fortunate sublimation of their proclivity toward magical identifications with others. Many great actors have been individuals without well-formed egos and with rather colorless though amiable ("as-if") personalities. (In all fairness, however, it should be acknowledged that many other equally talented actors possess well-integrated characters.) The energetic and self-assured entrepreneurial attitude of individuals with *hypomanic personality disorder* often places them in social leadership roles where even their meddlesome tendencies are tolerated by others. *Antisocial personalities* too, especially those with no grossly criminal tendencies, can achieve striking socio-economic success. Certain *schizoid personalities* become successful in solitary intellectual work, such as hard research and literary pursuits. The schizoid individuals' attraction for literary and artistic activities is in part due to the fact that such activities provide an exhibitionistic means of expression without involving genuine spontaneity and direct interpersonal contact. *Paranoid individuals* may excel in politics and law, finding a socially acceptable expression of their inherent cynicism and combativeness in these professions. Some of their traits, especially grandiosity, mistrustful aloofness, and hair-splitting oratorical skills might lead them into becoming fanatical preachers and cult leaders. Their not infrequently disastrous downfall from these positions of power is often preceded by considerable social recognition and fame. Even the obviously impaired *borderline individuals* may be capable of important artistic and literary contributions.

Low social functioning and the existence of a severe personality disorder are therefore not correlated on a one-to-one basis. Factors other than character pathology also determine social functioning. These include the presence of natural talents, intelligence, socioeconomic background, fortunate "breaks," education, and the impact of significant extrafamilial later identifications in the form of teachers, neighbors, clergy, vocational mentors, and so on. This whole area of the relationship between the level of character organization and social functioning, however, is ill understood and merits further investigation.

SUGGESTED READINGS

Akhtar, S. (1992). *Broken Structures: Severe Personality Disorders and Their Treatment*. Northvale, NJ: Jason Aronson.

Diagnostic and Statistical Manual of Mental Disorders (1980). 3rd ed., p. 318. Washington, DC: American Psychiatric Association.

Kernberg, O. F. (1975). *Borderline Conditions and Pathological Narcissism*, pp. 229–230, 252–255. New York: Jason Aronson.

15. Do admixtures between various severe personality disorders exist?

Indeed. Clinical experience demonstrates that *patients often present with features of more than one severe personality disorder at a time.* Actually, this is to be expected. The common developmental substrate (e.g., aborted separation-individuation, lack of object constancy, persistence of splitting mechanisms, distorted Oedipus complex) of the various types of such psychopathology results in their having overlapping phenomenological pictures.

Narcissistic personality disorder, for instance, overlaps with paranoid, hypomanic, and antisocial characters. Like paranoid personality, it has a facade of cold grandiosity, restrained affectivity, chronic envy, and an undue sense of entitlement. Like hypomanic personality, it displays grandiosity, articulateness, seductiveness, love of big schemes, and moral, aesthetic, and vocational enthusiasm. Like antisocial personality, it might indulge in substance abuse, promiscuity, lying, manipulativeness, and morally questionable behavior. These overlaps are not insignificant. At the same time, enough differences between narcissistic personality and the other three disorders exist to allow its distinction from them.

The same applies to other severe personality disorders. Take the example of borderline personality disorder, which has phenomenological overlaps on the one hand with histrionic personality, and on the other hand with schizotypal personality. Like histrionic personality, it shows a clinging attitude, readiness for regression, manipulativeness, and constant need for attention. Like schizotypal personality, it displays vulnerability to magical thinking, ideas of reference, and oddities of communication. Once again, however, enough differences exist between borderline and the other two conditions to allow its distinction from them. Similar admixtures and overlaps exist between paranoid and schizoid, paranoid and antisocial, schizoid and schizotypal, and histrionic and antisocial personality disorders.

In conceptualizing such admixture, one option is to diagnose all individuals with such hybrid conditions as having a "mixed personality disorder." Such a permissive category is, however, likely to end up as a nosological wastebasket and fuel diagnostic sloppiness. Another option is to insist upon strict categorical separation between various severe personality disorders and assign more than one personality disorder label to cases with mixed features; indeed, this practice might account for the well-documented problem of inordinate overlap among many of the *DSM-III-R* criteria sets for specific personality disorders. Clearly, separating various personality disorders to such a degree is not supported by clinical realities. A final and more meaningful option is to use the diagnostic profiles only as friendly guideposts and not inviolable categories. In this approach, mixed pictures are almost the rule and the diagnosis of a specific personality disorder is not based upon a total exclusion of the features of another personality disorder but on the predominance of those for the entity under consideration.

SUGGESTED READINGS

Akhtar, S. (1991). Three fantasies related to unresolved separation-individuation: a less recognized aspect of severe character pathology. In *Beyond the Symbiotic Orbit: Advances in Separation-Individuation Theory—Essays in Honor of Selma Kramer, M.D.*, ed. S. Akhtar and H. Parens, pp. 261–284. Hillsdale, NJ: Analytic Press.

Pfohl, B., Coryell, W., Zimmerman, M., et al. (1986). *DSM-III* personality disorders: diagnostic overlap and internal consistency of individual *DSM-III* criteria. *Comprehensive Psychiatry* 27: 21–34.

Siever, L., and Klar, H. (1986). A review of *DSM-III* criteria for the personality disorders. In *Psychiatry Update: American Psychiatric Association Annual Review*, vol. 5, ed. A. Frances, R. Hales, pp. 279–314. Washington, DC: American Psychiatric Press.

Part II

STRUCTURE AND DYNAMICS

16. What is *identity*?

The term *identity* was introduced into psychoanalytic literature by Victor Tausk (1919), who examined how the child discovers his self and asserted that man must, throughout life, constantly find himself anew. It was, however, Erik Erikson who offered the most thorough exposition of the concept of identity. Significant contributions were later made by Heinz Lichtenstein, Phyllis Greenacre, Edith Jacobson, Margaret Mahler, Otto Kernberg, and Peter Blos.

Erikson (1956) used the term *ego identity* to denote "both a persistent sameness within oneself (self-sameness) and a persistent sharing of same kind of essential character with others" (p. 57). He later dropped the word *ego* in order to accommodate Hartmann's differentiation between ego and self. Erikson emphasized that identity had many connotations, including a conscious sense of individuality, an unconscious striving for continuity of personal character, and an inner solidarity with a group's ideals. Erikson's later writings contain two views of identity: *ego identity* that results from self-objectification, and *existential identity* that is defined by the relationship of each soul to its mere existence.

Lichtenstein also held that the conflict between identity as self-objectification and identity as pure existential awareness without any external referent has to be accepted as such. He proposed two opposing forces as being active in connection with identity: *identity principle* and *metamorphosis*. The first originates in the symbiotic mother–child relationship and reflects the perpetual drive of man to assert and maintain his historical existence and unique individuality. The second originates in the autistic core of the self and involves a longing to abandon the human quality of identity. Lichtenstein sees human life as existing in an oscillation between the two extremes of identity and metamorphosis.

Subsequent investigations have upheld the view that identity originates in the earliest mother–infant interactions, with the development of body image at the core of identity formation. This begins in the symbiotic phase and gains momentum as the separation-individuation process unfolds. Identity obtains its structural substrate from primitive introjections; refines itself through differentiation from early objects; is strengthened by more selective later identifications; assumes a basic bisexual flavor through identification with parents of both sexes; acquires filiation, generational boundaries, and temporality in the passage through the Oedipus complex; and arrives at its more or less final shape during adolescence through greater individuation, renunciation of negative oedipal strivings, and synthesis of contradictory identifications resulting in a predominance of identification with the parent of the same sex.

A well-established identity consists of (1) sustained self-sameness, (2) display of roughly similar character traits in varied social contexts, (3) realistic body image, (4) temporal continuity in the self-experience, (5) authenticity, (6) clarity regarding one's gender and preponderance of same sex identifications, (7) enduring sense of inner fullness and the associated capacity for peaceful aloneness, (8) well-internalized conscience, and (9) inner solidarity with a familial and ethnic group's ideals.

SUGGESTED READINGS

Erikson, E. H. (1956). The problem of ego identity. *Journal of the American Psychoanalytic Association* 4:56–121.

Lichtenstein, H. (1963). The dilemma of human identity: notes on self transformation, self-objectivation, and metamorphosis. *Journal of the American Psychoanalytic Association* 11:173–223.

Moore, B. E., and Fine, B. D., eds. (1990). *Psychoanalytic Terms and Concepts*, pp. 92–93. New Haven, CT: Yale University Press.

17. What are the manifestations of identity diffusion?

Identity diffusion, originally described by Erikson in 1950 and later elaborated upon by Jacobson, Mahler, Kernberg, and me, denotes a more or less characteristic constellation of the following manifestations.

(1) *Contradictory character traits*: Individuals with identity diffusion display seemingly incompatible personality traits: tenderness and indifference, naïveté and mistrust, greed and asceticism, shyness and exhibitionism, timidity and arrogance, and so on. The lack of an integrated self-concept is associated with impaired integration of the concept of others. Lacking this normal requisite for empathy, individuals with identity diffusion need to focus excessively on the immediate behavior of others in order to "read" them.

(2) *Temporal discontinuity*: The past, present, and future are not integrated for such individuals in a smooth continuum of remembered, felt, and expected existence. This chronological rupture manifests as an inability to project oneself into future roles, a striking nonchalance about past loyalties to individuals and places, vocational zigzags, and, in older patients, a peculiar dissociation from their own younger selves.

(3) *Lack of authenticity*: Identity diffusion is accompanied by lack of genuineness and vulnerability to acquiring gestures, phrases, ideologies, and lifestyles from others. This tendency towards mimicry is based upon need-driven malleability vis-à-vis external environment as well as upon the inner presence of unsynthesized early introjections.

(4) *Subtle body image disturbances*: Individuals with identity diffusion lack a realistic body image and do not have a comfortable somatic foundation to their self-experience. They make erroneous assessments of their height, weight, complexion, voice,

and so on. The body rigidity of borderline, the thermal sensitivity of narcissistic, and the motor clumsiness of schizoid personalities are examples of such disturbed psychosomatic partnership.

(5) *Feelings of emptiness*: Identity diffusion leads to a feeling of inner emptiness that is especially marked during actual aloneness. Emptiness is characterized by absence of fantasy and longing. It is a dehumanizing and frightening experience. To ward it off, many individuals remain constantly active and incessantly social. Promiscuity, bulimia, substance abuse, and provocative behavior that ultimately "fills" one up with rage might also serve a similar defensive purpose.

(6) *Gender dysphoria*: Individuals with identity diffusion have weak core gender identity, unresolved bisexuality and difficulties with heterosexuality. They might display overt behaviors typical of the opposite sex, or they may fail to convey a deep sense of possessing any gender at all, thus displaying a state of psychic eunuchoidism.

(7) *Inordinate ethnic and moral relativism*: In such individuals, there is also a pallor of ethnicity. They have a vague and uneven sense of history, generational continuity, cultural norms, group affiliations, lifestyle, and child-rearing practices. Their conscience displays an exaggerated latitude and surprising contradictions.

Identity diffusion is present in all severe personality disorders. However, the degree to which it is readily manifest varies and its differing manifestations do not occur to an equal degree in all types of patients.

SUGGESTED READINGS

Akhtar, S. (1984). The syndrome of identity diffusion. *American Journal of Psychiatry* 141:1381–1385.

Erikson, E. H. (1950). Growth and crises of the healthy personality. In *Identity and the Life Cycle*, pp. 50–100. New York: International Universities Press.

Kernberg, O. F. (1967). Borderline personality organization. *Journal of the American Psychoanalytic Association* 15:641–685.

18. How does identity diffusion differ from adolescent identity crisis?

Identity crisis denotes an intensified form of the phase-specific and expectable resurgence of doubts, regression in behavior, and reorganization of identity during adolescence. This developmental phase, with its characteristic drive upsurge, fosters regression. Adolescents tend to retreat from oedipal conflicts and seek refuge in struggles over control, autonomy, and distance. Regressive tendencies intensify primary self- and object relations. Progressive trends herald new self-configurations and loosening of infantile object ties. On the one hand, there is insistent disengagement from the earlier parental mores internalized in the form of the superego. On the other hand, there is an equally strong reliance on the values of one's peers and contemporaries. Trial identifications and role experimentations within the latter context gradually broaden the ego autonomy and help consolidate a resilient, mature self-representation.

In distinguishing adolescent identity crisis from identity diffusion, Kernberg emphasized the absence of chronic, deep-seated pathology of internal object relationships in the former condition. Even during behavioral chaos, adolescents manage to retain authenticity and the capacity to view others with ambivalence rather than as caricatures of good and evil. Their idealizations, though intense, are often based upon a surprisingly deep knowledge of their heroes. Also, their heroes are temporary way stations to actual object investments and not substitutes for the latter. Their conflicts revolve around their psychosocial roles, distance from parents, and establishment of sexuality. They do not display defects of core gender identity, and, while at times lonely, do not experience dehumanizing emptiness.

Identity diffusion, on the other hand, implies severe psychopathology. Developmentally, identity diffusion is a consequence of a failed separation-individuation process (resulting in faulty self- and object constancy), unresolved Oedipus complex (re-sulting in faulty filiation and defective superego), and failure during adolescence to integrate earlier identifications into a uni-fied, enduring, and stable self-representation. Dynamically, iden-tity diffusion signifies the continued active presence of unmetabolized introjects and contradictory identifications, as well as the predominance of splitting over repression as a defense against object-related ambivalence and ego-dystonic self-attributes. Individuals with identity diffusion lack a realistic body image and have poorly formed selves. Their idealizations are fantastic and based on meager knowledge of their heroes; often such idealizations substitute for investment in actual objects. Their capacity for tolerating ambivalence is severely compro-mised. Superego functions are archaic, contradictory, and often felt as emanating from the environment rather than from within the self. The dependence on external objects for a cohesive self-feeling is great, leading to a vulnerability to the subjective experience of emptiness.

Both identity crisis and identity diffusion might become manifest during adolescence. However, the symptoms of identity diffusion are not restricted to that age and may be seen in adults of all ages. Also, although identity crisis can occur during the adolescence of relatively normal and/or neurotic individuals, identity diffusion betrays a borderline personality organization.

SUGGESTED READINGS

Blos, P. (1967). The second individuation process of adolescence. *Psychoanalytic Study of the Child* 22:162–186. New York: International Universities Press.

Erikson, E. (1950). Growth and crises of the healthy personality. In *Identity and the Life Cycle*, pp. 50–100. New York: International Universities Press.

Kernberg, O. F. (1978). The diagnosis of borderline conditions in adolescence. *Adolescent Psychiatry* 6:298–319.

19. Is *borderline personality disorder* the same as *borderline personality organization?*

No. *Borderline personality disorder* is a phenomenological designation that refers to a specific psychiatric syndrome. After brewing long on the back burners of psychiatric nosology, this concept received impetus from John Gunderson's work in the 1970s and widespread recognition by its inclusion in *DSM-III* in 1980. Borderline personality disorder is characterized by diffuse impulsivity, chronic anger, unstable and intense interpersonal relationships that shift between idealization and devaluation, identity disturbance, affective instability, feelings of boredom and emptiness, and a proclivity toward self-destructive acts.

Borderline personality organization, in contrast, is a psychostructural concept with certain developmental implications and a specific location in the hierarchy of character organization. Introduced into the psychoanalytic lexicon by Kernberg in 1967, borderline personality organization refers to a character structure with identity diffusion, predominance of splitting over repression as the ego's main defensive operation, and an arrested separation-individuation process (with the resultant lack of self- and object constancy), much pregenital aggression, and marked preoedipal coloration to the Oedipus complex.

The inner world characteristic of borderline personality organization is populated by dissociated ego segments, each of which contains a self-image, a part-object image, and an affect disposition. Although differentiation between self and object is intact, the self experience is far from coherent. Oscillations between extremely favorable or unfavorable estimations of the self are frequent. Capacity for comprehending objects in their richly textured totality is impaired. Affects pertaining to ambivalence, mourning, and genuine sadness are deficient. Superego integration is minimal. Internalized bad object images, forming superego forerunners of a sadistic kind, are easily projected, creating frightening external persecutors. Overidealized self- and object images create fantastically high, unachievable ideals, which fail to provide benevolent inner guidance.

Kernberg also highlighted the typical constellations of preoedipally distorted oedipal conflicts in borderline personality organization. These include (1) an excessive aggressivation of oedipal conflicts, (2) an undue idealization of love relations, whether homo- or heterosexual, (3) a highly unrealistic quality to the fantasied relations with either the positive or negative oedipal objects, (4) a pregenital agenda to seemingly genital strivings, and (5) a premature oedipalization of preoedipal conflicts.

Kernberg's borderline personality organization does not refer to a discrete nosological entity but to the psychic substrate of all severe personality disorders. Clearly, then, the concepts of borderline personality disorder and borderline personality organization are on different levels of abstraction although they do overlap in some ways. *A borderline personality organization underlies all cases of borderline personality disorder. However, not all cases of borderline personality organizations present as borderline personality disorder.* Borderline personality organization also underlies narcissistic, paranoid, schizoid, antisocial, and hypomanic personality disorders, and certain cases of alcoholism, drug abuse, and sexual perversions.

SUGGESTED READINGS

Gunderson, J. G., and Singer, M. (1975). Defining borderline patients: an overview. *American Journal of Psychiatry* 133:1–10.

Kernberg, O. F. (1967). Borderline personality organization. *Journal of the American Psychoanalytic Association* 15:641–685.

Perry, J. C., and Klerman, G. L. (1978). The borderline patient. *Archives of General Psychiatry* 35:141–150.

20. What is the *grandiose self*?

The term *grandiose self* owes its origin to Heinz Kohut who first used it in his now renowned book *The Analysis of the Self* (1971). Kohut used the designation for the "grandiose and exhibitionistic image of the self" (p. 25) typically found in individuals with narcissistic personality disorder. A common consequence of such a psychic structure is relentless pursuit of perfection and constant need for acclaim. This is frequently associated with a depletion of the ego. The grandiose self impairs the mature functioning of the ego, and its archaic claims repeatedly intrude upon the realistic activities of the individual. A truly talented person's ego "may well be pushed to the use of its utmost capacities, and thus to a realistically outstanding performance, by the demands of the grandiose fantasies of a persistent, poorly modified grandiose self" (p. 109). Less gifted individuals, however, can only manage a caricature of this situation. Under the sway of the omnipotent claims of the grandiose self, they often are unable to ask for needed information, fail to admit lacunae in their knowledge, display subtle learning defects, and are vulnerable to lying in order to hide their real and imagined deficiencies.

Kohut proposed that under optimally empathic developmental conditions, the grandiose self typical of childhood is gradually tamed and becomes integrated into the adult personality. It then supplies the force behind ego-syntonic goals and realistic ambitions. However, if the child suffers severe narcissistic traumas, then the grandiose self does not become assimilated into the ego and persists unaltered, constantly striving for the fulfillment of its primitive aims. The activation of such grandiose self during psychoanalysis is the basis of the *mirror transference* described by Kohut. Regressive movements from a cohesive mirror transference bring forth even more archaic grandiosity. This might manifest as cold and imperious behavior, affected speech, and claims of unrealistic grandiose feats. Greater regression than this leads to hypochondria, varieties of self stimulating behaviors, and perverse sexuality. Narcissistic injuries occurring outside the context of analytic treatment can also usher in regressions from a cohesive grandiose self.

In contrast to Kohut, Kernberg uses the term *grandiose self* not to describe the normal narcissism of childhood but for a psychic structure that is pathological to begin with. Borrowing Kohut's term, he proposes a different etiological and structural formulation for it. Kernberg proposes that the grandiose self is formed by the fusion of (1) the actually praiseworthy and special aspects of the self, (2) an idealized self-image (containing the fantasies of glory and power that protected the small child against feeling frustrated and angry), and (3) an ideal object representation (the fantasied ever-loving, ever-giving parent). At the same time, the aggressively tinged self- and object representations are split off and externalized. One thus appears "all good" to oneself.

> The integration of this pathological, grandiose self compensates for the lack of integration of the normal self-concept which is part of the underlying borderline personality organization: it explains the paradox of relatively good ego functioning and surface adaptation in the presence of a predominance of splitting mechanisms, a related constellation of primitive defenses, and the lack of integration of object representations of these patients. [Kernberg 1975, p. 266]

There are two main distinctions between Kohut's and Kernberg's views on grandiose self. Kohut regards it as a fixation upon an archaic but normal psychic structure of childhood. Kernberg believes that it reflects a pathological structure distinct from normal childhood narcissism. Moreover, Kohut believes the rage of such persons to be a response to their grandiose selves being injured, whereas Kernberg sees their rage as the inciting agent for the very formation of the grandiose self.

SUGGESTED READINGS

Akhtar, S. (1989). Kohut and Kernberg: a critical comparison. In *Self Psychology: Comparisons and Contrasts*, ed. D. W. Detrick and S. P. Detrick, pp. 329–362. Hillsdale, NJ: Analytic Press.

Kernberg, O. F. (1975). *Borderline Conditions and Pathological Narcissism*, pp. 263–314. New York: Jason Aronson.

Kohut, H. (1971). *The Analysis of the Self*. New York: International Universities Press.

21. What is *malignant narcissism*?

The grandiose self in narcissistic personality disorder is usually built around the libidinal self- and object-representations. By introjective identification, the desirable aspects of others are claimed as belonging to oneself and by projective identification, unacceptable aspects of the self are deposited into others. The actual good aspects of the self (e.g., an inherent talent) are made to hypertrophy by relentless effort. An idealized self-image is maintained and anything challenging it is vehemently defended against. The individual feels he is (or should be) loved by everyone because he is so lovable. Such an individual feels threatened by discovering goodness in others and defends against envy by devaluing them, attempting to control them, or avoiding contact with them altogether.

Herbert Rosenfeld described a more disturbing form of narcissistic personality where *grandiosity is built around aggression and the destructive aspects of the self become idealized.* Such patients seek to destroy whatever love is offered them in order to maintain their superiority over others. In becoming totally identified with the omnipotent destructive aspects of their selves and their internalized bad objects, they kill off their sane and loving selves, which could develop attachment and dependence. At times, they are wistfully aware of their inner imprisonment but feel that there is little anybody (or they themselves) can do to change this Faustian bondage.

Developing such ideas further, Otto Kernberg introduced the term *malignant narcissism* into psychoanalytic literature in 1984. He used this designation to describe a characteristic condensation of grandiose and sadistic strivings in some narcissistic patients. Kernberg outlined four features of this syndrome: (1) a typical narcissistic personality disorder, (2) antisocial behavior, (3) ego-syntonic sadism, and (4) a deeply paranoid orientation toward life. Individuals with malignant narcissism consistently attempt to destroy, symbolically castrate, and dehumanize others. Their m is often expressed in ideological terms. They can become leaders of religious cults and terrorist groups. Within the context of these settings, they might display the ability for concern and loyalty to their peers and followers; this distinguishes them from individuals with antisocial personality proper. They can also have ego-syntonic suicidal tendencies that do not reflect sadness and inner guilt but a megalomanic triumph over the ordinary fear of pain and death, leading them to become "victim and victimizer in one" (Kernberg 1984, p. 292). Their paranoid tendencies manifest in their viewing others as enemies or fools and their preoccupation with conspiracies and, if they happen to be religious fanatics, with Armageddon. Their paranoid beliefs fuel their antisocial behavior and the untoward consequences of such actions lend justification to their pervasive mistrust.

Patients with malignant narcissism are very difficult to treat. In the therapeutic situation, they typically display "(1) paranoid regression in the transference, including 'paranoid micropsychotic episodes'; (2) chronic self destructiveness or suicide as a triumph over the analyst; (3) major or minor dishonesty in the transference; and (4) overt sadistic triumph over the analyst, or malignant grandiosity" (Kernberg 1984, p. 290). The outcome of therapeutic efforts in such cases depends upon the patient's remaining capacity for attachment and for maintaining a therapeutic situation in the midst of severe negative transference as well as upon the availability of treatment arrangements structured to prevent suicidal and sadistic acting out.

SUGGESTED READINGS

Kernberg, O. F. (1984). *Severe Personality Disorders*. New Haven, CT: Yale University Press.

———— (1989). The narcissistic personality disorder and the differential diagnosis of antisocial behavior. *The Psychiatric Clinics of North America* 12:553–570.

Rosenfeld, H. (1971). Theory of life and death instincts: aggressive aspects of narcissism. *International Journal of Psycho-Analysis* 45:332–337.

22. What does the term *false self* denote?

The term *false self* was introduced into the psychoanalytic nomenclature by Donald Winnicott in 1960. Winnicott acknowledged that the concept itself was not new, having existed in various guises in psychiatric, religious, and philosophical systems. At the same time, he gave a sharper and richer connotation to the term. According to Winnicott, the origin of false self is in the earliest infant–mother interactions. The infant, in the beginning, is psychologically unintegrated though he periodically expresses a spontaneous gesture. If the mother makes sense out of this gesture and thus meets the infant's omnipotence, then what is potentially real and authentic (the *true self*) in the infant begins to have life. If, on the other hand, the mother repeatedly fails to implement the infant's omnipotence and decode his gesture and substitutes her own gesture, which is to be given sense by the infant, his *true self* withdraws inwardly and he is forced into compliance. "This compliance on the part of the infant is the earliest stage of the false self, and belongs to the mother's inability to sense her infant's needs" (Winnicott 1960, p. 145). Winnicott went on to state that such an infant (and later, child) begins to live falsely, that is, without genuine spontaneity. "Compliance is then the main feature, with imitation as a specialty" (p. 147). Winnicott classified the subsequent adult false self organizations into five hierarchically arranged categories:

(1) *The false self sets itself up as the real personality*, though in situations that demand genuineness and depth others can notice that something essential is missing (see also Helene Deutsch's description of the *as if* personality in this regard).

(2) *The false self defends the true self*, which is allowed a secret life. The false self therefore ensures the preservation of the individual in spite of abnormal environmental conditions.

(3) *The false self searches for conditions in which the true self can be allowed a safe emergence.* "If such conditions can not be found then there must be reorganized a new defence against

exploitation of the true self, and if there be doubt then the clinical result is suicide. Suicide in this context is the destruction of the total self in avoidance of annihilation the true self" (Winnicott 1960, p. 143).

(4) *The false self is built on identifications.* Here, Winnicott seems to be implying a preponderance of defensive identifications that might not be in sync with one's inherent potential and aptitudes.

(5) *The false self is represented by good manners and a polite social attitude.* A healthy individual, too, needs a bit of false self; his true self alone is not entirely suitable for gaining a place in society.

Winnicott emphasized that these conceptualizations have technical consequences, especially for the analyst's recognizing the pseudo-alliance and inauthentic compliance of such patients, which hide a deep dread of (and, underlying it, a wish for) profound dependence. Otherwise the treatment goes on endlessly with little actual gain.

While Winnicott's notions are poignant and useful, *a word of caution* is in order. The false self organization is not to be deduced merely from the patient's claim, however plaintive, of feeling fraudulent and impostrous. Such inauthenticity is not infrequently a defensive retreat from the potential anxiety and guilt about being solidly oneself. In general, inauthenticity is a complex phenomenon with various determinants. No unitary explanation is applicable to all cases.

SUGGESTED READINGS

Deutsch, H. (1942). Some forms of emotional disturbance and their relationship to schizophrenia. *Psychoanalytic Quarterly* 11:301–321.

Gediman, H. K. (1985). Impostor, inauthenticity, and feeling fraudulent. *Journal of the American Psychoanalytic Association* 33:911–936.

Winnicott, D. W. (1960). Ego distortion in terms of true and false self. In *The Maturational Processes* and *The Facilitating Environment*, pp. 140–152. New York: International Universities Press, 1965.

23. Do all severe personality disorders have superego defects?

Yes. Defects of superego are invariably present in all forms of severe character pathology. These defects involve the strength of superego, its coherence and consistency, its vulnerability to externalization, the extent of its depersonification, and its demarcation from the other psychic structures. Such close association of severe character pathology and superego defects should not be surprising at all. Indeed, it is to be expected.

The formation of a healthy and effectively functioning superego is contingent upon a number of factors including (1) constitutional integrity (and subsequent continued freedom from conflict) of the primary autonomous ego functions; (2) neutralization of pregenital drives with dominance of libido over aggression; (3) achievement of self- and object constancy, and along with it the renunciation of infantile omnipotence, forward projection of narcissism, and capacity for idealizing the parents; (4) a sustained and affectively significant oedipal experience followed by its resolution, resulting in prototypical intrapsychic incest barrier and dominance of heterosexual identifications; (5) the capacity for role-based, selective, and partial identifications; and, (6) further depersonification of early identifications, as well as a deeper renunciation of negative oedipal strivings leading to the consolidation of ego ideal during adolescence. These developmental steps for achieving a well-integrated, firm yet benevolent, and consistent inner conscience have not been optimally traversed by individuals with severe character pathology. Consequently, their superego is almost always riddled with defects and inconsistencies.

A quick glance at the symptomatology of various personality disorders (narcissistic, borderline, paranoid, antisocial, hypomanic, histrionic or infantile, schizoid, schizotypal, and "as-if") confirms such a view. The most severe superego defect is, of course, associated with *antisocial* personality disorder. Individuals with this disorder typically show extreme self-centeredness, re-markable absence of concern for others, parasitism, incapacity for self-reflective sadness, total absence of guilt, and a tendency toward active or passive criminality. Other severe personality disorders also show superego defects, though these are less intense and less pervasive. *Narcissistic* and *hypomanic* individuals show a subtle readiness to shift values to gain favor, irreverence toward authority, tendency to cut ethical corners and, not infrequently, pathological lying. *Borderline* individuals can also be corruptible, parasitic, ruthlessly exploitative, and given to lying, stealing, and impulsive criminal acts. Their superego integration is minimal and its sadistic forerunners are readily externalized. Moreover, the delimitations between ego and ego ideal and between ego and superego are blurred. Consequently, such patients do not respond to a real or imagined reprimand by feeling that they *did* something bad but by feeling that they *are* bad. Similarly, they respond to a real or imagined reward not by feeling that the act involved has been good, but that they as persons are great. As a result, borderline individuals are vulnerable to both megalomanic exal-tations and devastating self-loathing. Vulnerability to passive criminality, parasitism, and promiscuity in *as-if* and *histrionic* individuals, odd fluctuations between striking altruism and amo-rality, as well as vulnerability to intense mystical and parapsycho-logical phenomena in *schizoid* and *schizotypal* characters, and a tendency for expedient mendacity and treacherousness in *para-noid* personalities constitute other phenomenological examples of superego pathology in severe personality disorders.

SUGGESTED READINGS

Akhtar, S. (1992). *Broken Structures: Severe Personality Disorders and Their Treatment*. Northvale, NJ: Jason Aronson.

Eissler, K. R., ed. (1949). *Searchlights on Delinquency: Essays in Honor of August Aichhorn*. New York: International Universities Press.

Kernberg, O. F. (1989). The narcissistic personality disorder and the differential diagnosis of antisocial behavior. *The Psychiatric Clinics of North America* 12:533–570.

24. What are the manifestations of ego weakness?

Ego weakness refers to deficits in the capacity to negotiate between the demands of external reality on the one hand and instinctual urges and superego dictates on the other. A strong ego is one that can successfully accomplish this task. An individual with such an ego can control inner impulses and tolerate increases in anxiety without regression, symptom formation, or action. He or she can also channel instinctual urges into morally acceptable and realistically safe forms of discharge. A weak ego shows deficiencies in these areas.

Kernberg divides the manifestations of ego weakness into two categories: those "specific" to lower levels of character organization and those which are "nonspecific" signs of ego weakness. Among the former, he includes (1) *blurring of ego boundaries*, and (2) *predominance of primitive defenses*. A weak ego has ill-defined boundaries, which result in shaky reality testing and difficulty in discerning the source of one's affects, ideas, and impulses, whether these are originating from within oneself or in external objects. There is a lack of clarity between conceptual and perceptual, internal and external, and fantasized and real aspects of any given experience. A weak ego is also characterized by the use of primitive defenses (splitting, projective identification, denial, primitive idealization, etc.). The use of splitting is especially marked. Since splitting "requires less countercathexis than repression, a weak ego falls back easily on splitting, and a vicious cycle is created by which ego weakness and splitting reinforce each other" (Kernberg 1975, p. 29). Projective identification, another significant primitive ego defense, also weakens ego boundaries, especially in the area of managing aggression.

Among the nonspecific manifestations of ego weakness, Kernberg includes three characteristics: (1) *lack of anxiety tolerance*, (2) *poor impulse control*, and (3) *impaired capacity for sublimation*. Lack of anxiety tolerance is reflected by the extent to which any additional quantum of anxiety leads the individual toward regression, symptom formation, or discharge through action. The actually plausible as opposed to the totally unrealistic nature of fantasies triggered by an additional load of anxiety perhaps also reflect ego strength and ego weakness respectively. Lack of impulse control manifests either as structured impulsivity (focal, repetitive, ego-syntonic, and subsequently shrugged-off specific acts) characteristically associated with splitting, or a diffuse, erratic, and unpredictable loss of restraint upon inner urges and desires. Lack of developed sublimatory channels is also a manifestation of ego weakness. The absence of areas of deep interest and an adequate work record, deficient capacity for pleasurable pursuit of hobbies, and impaired creativity and playfulness all indicate poverty of sublimation. In assessing this area of ego functioning, however, it is important to keep the individual's socio-cultural background in mind.

> In a highly stimulating, culture-oriented social environment the lack of enjoyment and creativity of the borderline patient may be obscured by his surface adaptation to that optimal environment. In contrast, patients chronically submerged in a socially severely deprived environment may appear as bland, joyless, and uncreative superficially, without necessarily revealing the more severe aspects of lack of sublimatory capacity on a deeper level. [Kernberg 1975, p. 23]

The concept of ego weakness is significant not only for diagnostic purposes but also for selecting a treatment strategy. Patients who retain relatively stable areas of ego strength, even if otherwise borderline, might be suitable for psychoanalysis. Patients who show pervasive ego weakness, in contrast, require much more structured psychotherapeutic interventions, ranging from psychoanalytic psychotherapy to supportive management.

SUGGESTED READINGS

Fenichel, O. (1954). Ego strength and ego weakness. In *Collected Papers*, vol. 2, pp. 25–48. New York: Norton.

Kernberg, O. F. (1975). *Borderline Conditions and Pathological Narcissism*, pp. 22–24, New York: Jason Aronson.

Moore, B. E., and Fine, B. D. (1990). *Psychoanalytic Terms and Concepts*, p. 66. New Haven, CT: Yale University Press.

25. What is meant by *primitive ego defenses?*

The word *primitive* is applied to ego defenses in three different contexts. The first is a *developmental* one. It proposes that certain ego defenses are utilized very early in life, while others do not appear until a greater degree of ego organization is evident. Such chronological hierarchy of defenses was first noted by Anna Freud (1936), who stated that "each defense mechanism is first evolved in order to master some specific instinctual urge and so is associated with a particular phase of infantile development" (p. 51). Denial, regression, ego restriction, and turning against the self appear earlier in the course of development than repression, rationalization, and sublimation. Projection and introjection are also later in the developmental hierarchy, since their working depends upon the differentiation of the ego from the outside world. Melanie Klein and Margaret Mahler's analytic work with children lent further support to the idea of such a hierarchy. Klein described the defenses of splitting of the ego and its objects, introjection, projection, projective identification, denial of inner reality, idealization, and omnipotence. These mechanisms come into operation at the earliest infantile stage (the *paranoid-schizoid position*) and failure to renounce their use leads to the inability to achieve the next, more mature, psychic organization (the *depressive position*). Consequently, there remains a lifelong vulnerability to fall back on these earlier defenses. Mahler, too, described many of these mechanisms, especially splitting of the self- and object representations, as characteristic of the first two years of life, after which repression takes over as the chief defensive operation.

The second context in which the term primitive ego defenses is used is a *motivational* one. Frosch, for instance, differentiates between primitive and mature defenses on the basis of the type of psychic danger that necessitates their use. He proposes that separation anxiety, castration anxiety, and guilt mobilize defenses such as repression, reaction formation, rationalization, conversion, and displacement. More profound dangers to the ego, such as threats to self constancy or loss of identity, however, mobilize splitting, regressive loss of boundaries, introjective-projective maneuvers, projective identification, denial, and somatization.

Finally, the expression primitive ego defenses has a *diagnostic* connotation. Here, Fairbairn's analytic work with schizoid patients is important and so is Kernberg's scheme of the hierarchical levels of character organization. Kernberg (1970) asserts that individuals with a lower level of character organization (which includes all severe personality disorders) use defenses that are different from those used at a higher level of character organization (e.g., obsessional, hysterical, ego-syntonically phobic, and wildly masochistic characters). These primitive defenses include splitting, projective identification, denial, primitive idealization, omnipotence, and devaluation. Kernberg traces the origin of these defenses to the latter part of the first year and the second year of life after which, under normal circumstances, they are increasingly replaced by repression and other related defenses, for example, rationalization, projection, reaction formation, and so on.

Clearly, these developmental, motivational, and diagnostic contexts overlap. It seems that primitive ego defenses are those that appear early in life, that deal with deeper and more fundamental anxieties about self and object ties, and whose persistence into adult life is associated with severe character pathology. While this seems generally accepted, it should be acknowledged in all fairness that a contrary sentiment also exists. According to this view (Willick 1983), there are no specific primitive ego defenses. All kinds of defenses might be used by all kinds of people, and it is more important to have a broader assessment of ego functioning than to look for specific defenses suggesting more or less severe psychopathology.

SUGGESTED READINGS

Freud, A. (1936). *The Ego and the Mechanisms of Defense.* New York: International Universities Press, 1966.

Kernberg, O. F. (1970). A psychoanalytic classification of character pathology. *Journal of the American Psychoanalytic Association* 15:641–685.

Willick, M. S. (1983). On the concept of primitive defenses. *Journal of the American Psychoanalytic Association* 31 (supplement):175–200.

26. What is splitting and what are its clinical manifestations?

The term *splitting* has a long and complex history in psychiatry and psychoanalysis. The phenomenological tradition of the late nineteenth and early twentieth centuries often employed related concepts such as "double conscience," "split personality," and "dissociation of psychic phenomena." The concept of splitting was further elaborated by Freud, who used the term in many ways. First, he spoke of "splitting of consciousness" to denote the alternating states of awareness in hysterical patients. Later, he noted "splitting of the ego" in the fetishist who simultaneously acknowledged and disavowed the absence of the penis in women. Still later, Freud noted the existence of two contrary and independent attitudes in psychoses. One takes account of reality and the other, under the influence of the instincts, detaches the ego from reality.

In contrast to these earlier usages, the current use of the term is in connection with severe personality disorders. This view was developed by psychoanalysts who followed Freud: Klein, Fairbairn, Kohut, Mahler, and Kernberg. The views of Mahler and Kernberg correspond well and are widely accepted. Mahler observed that the collapse of the toddler's omnipotence during the rapprochement subphase, coupled with emotional unavailability of the mother, creates hostile dependency on the mother. The resulting intense ambivalence calls for the defense of splitting. "Good" and "bad" mother images are kept apart, and aggression is turned against the self. This becomes the basis for habitually responding to stress with negative mood swings, as well as for the relentless pursuit of perfection in the self and/or others. According to Kernberg (1975), splitting begins as an inevitable means by which the infantile ego categorizes its pleasurable and unpleasurable experiences. Later, this same separation of "good" and "bad" self- and object representations can come to serve a defensive purpose against intense ambivalence. "This defensive division of the ego, in which what was at first a simple defect in integration is then used actively for other purposes, is in essence the mechanism of splitting" (p. 25). The use of splitting results in five clinical manifestations:

(1) *Inability to experience ambivalence*: Splitting leads to a division of objects into "all good" and "all bad" categories with the consequent inability to view them as having mixed qualities. Tendency toward idealization and devaluation follows from this.

(2) *Oscillations of self esteem*: The activation of contradictory self-representations by environmental cues leads to intense fluctuations of self-esteem. The contradictory feelings of being "all bad" and "all good" are experienced with comparable conviction and are not assimilated into a realistic self-view.

(3) *Intensificaiton of affects*: Intense emotions, including murderous rage, suicidal despair, worshiping awe, and megalomanic exaltation are readily experienced.

(4) *Impaired decision making*: The inability to view objects in their totality and the presence of intense affects play havoc with the cognitive processes involved in evaluating situations properly and weighing alternative courses of action. Consequently, decision making becomes impaired and is often reckless.

(5) *Ego-syntonic impulsivity*: Splitting also underlies a repetitive and ego-syntonic loss of impulse control (e.g., promiscuity, kleptomania) that produces little subsequent guilt, only a bland denial of its significance.

While better organized, neurotic level personalities might display occasional and focal splitting, its extensive use is a clinical marker of severe character pathology.

SUGGESTED READINGS

Akhtar, S., and Byrne, J. P. (1983). The concept of splitting and its clinical relevance. *American Journal of Psychiatry* 140:1013–1016.
Kernberg, O. F. (1975). *Borderline Conditions and Pathological Narcissism*, pp. 25–34. New York: Jason Aronson.
Mahler, M. S. (1974). Symbiosis and individuation: the psychological birth of the human infant. *Psychoanalytic Study of the Child* 29:89–106. New Haven, CT: Yale University Press.

27. What is *projective identification*?

The term *projective identification* was introduced into psychoanalytic literature by Melanie Klein in 1946. She described it as a process that begins in early infancy and consists of parts of the rudimentary self being split off and projected into an external object. The latter then becomes identified with the split-off part as well as possessed and internally controlled by it. While starting as a developmental process parallel to introjection, projective identification can later come to serve many defensive purposes. These include attempted fusion with an external object to avoid separation, control of internal bad objects that cause persecutory anxieties, and preservation of endangered good aspects of the self by depositing them into others. Although these conceptualizations were further elaborated by Klein's followers, especially Segal, Bion, and Rosenfeld, the term *projective identification* did not gain widespread acceptance in mainstream psychoanalysis, especially in the United States.

Kernberg's seminal work on borderline personality organization rejuvenated the concept. According to him, the individual using projective identification

> projects an intolerable intrapsychic experience onto an object, maintains empathy (in the sense of emotional awareness) with what he projects, tries to control the object in a continuing effort to defend against the intolerable experience, and unconsciously, in actual interaction with the object, leads the object to experience what has been projected onto him. [Kernberg 1992, p. 159]

Joseph Sandler, Thomas Ogden, and James Grotstein are among others who have elaborated the concept of projective identification.

Projective identification differs from projection, which is less primitive, does not involve blurring of ego boundaries, and causes a lesser need to manipulate the external object. The use of projective identification is associated with severe character pathology. Moreover, *the defense is a hybrid one, involving both intrapsychic and interpersonal aspects.* Essentially these consist of the repudiation of a self-representation, its attribution to another individual who can emotionally experience such induction, and an unconscious interpersonal manipulation of the latter so that he or she lives out the deposited aspect in reality. The concept of projective identification is valuable in deciphering countertransference experiences with borderline patients who deposit their dissociated aspects into their therapist and then pressure the latter to act it out. While a repudiation of unwanted aggressive self-representations (tinged with envy, greed, malice, etc.) has received more attention, Klein's notion that endangered good aspects can also be deposited into others for safekeeping still remains valid.

The importance of recognizing positive projective identification lies in both diagnostic and therapeutic realms. For instance, narcissistic individuals frequently deposit their inferiority and shame-laden self representations into others, causing them to experience such feelings. Schizoid individuals, on the other hand, deposit their optimistic and sane attributes into others for safekeeping and thus mobilize hope, curiosity, and rescue fantasies in the latter. Therapeutically, too, such conceptualization has significance. In the treatment of a severely self-loathing individual, for instance, the therapist takes a constructive step in gradually familiarizing the patient with a benevolent view of him. This good image of the patient inside the therapist is the result not only of the therapist's kindness but also of the patient's use of positive projective identification. The patient discovers this image, feels it, tries it out, and eventually makes it his own.

SUGGESTED READINGS

Kernberg, O. (1992). Projection and projective identification: developmental and clinical aspects. In *Aggression in Personality Disorders and Perversions*, pp. 159–172. New Haven, CT: Yale University Press.

Klein, M. (1946). Notes on some schizoid mechanisms. *International Journal of Psycho-Analysis* 27:99–110.

Sandler, J. (1987). The concept of projective identification. In *Projection, Identification, and Projective Identification*. Madison, CT: International Universities Press.

28. What does the term *manic defense* mean?

The term *manic defense* was first used by Melanie Klein in 1935. She described it as a set of mental mechanisms aimed at protecting the ego from depressive as well as paranoid anxieties. Klein described many forms of manic defense and often used the term in its plural form. Essentially, manic defense attempts to deny the psychic reality including the ego's "perilous dependence on its love objects" (Klein 1935, p. 277) and the danger with which it is menaced from its internalized bad objects. *Omnipotence, denial, and idealization are three typical constituents of manic defense.* Omnipotence is utilized to control and master objects, but without genuine concern for them. Denial is aimed at erasing the awareness of dependence upon others. Idealization (e.g., over-admiration, thinking in large numbers) tenaciously retains an "all good" view of the world and oneself which, in turn, defends against guilty recognition of having injured others, in fact or fantasy.

Winnicott emphasized that *manic defense is a measure against the experience of sadness and mourning.* In manic defense, relationships with external objects are used to decrease the tension in internal reality. Winnicott outlined four components of manic defense: (1) denial of internal reality, (2) flight to external reality from internal reality, (3) suspended animation, and (4) denial of depressive feelings. The denial of inner reality usually involves a repudiation of internalized bad objects but it might also send the good internal forces and objects into psychic exile. "Many who live normal and valuable lives do not feel they are responsible for the best that is in them" (Winnicott 1935, p. 133). Flight to external reality might involve frequent daydreaming, which interposes fantasy between the internal and external reality, as an intermediary step. Or, there might be an exploitation of sexuality and/or internal bodily sensations for avoiding internal reality. Employing the former, "the compulsive masturbator, abates psychic tension by the use of the satisfaction he got from autoerotic activity and from compulsive heterosexual or homosexual experiences, and [using] the latter, the hypochondriac, comes to tolerate psychic tension by denial of fantasy content" (p. 133). In the "suspended animation" aspect of manic defense, omnipotent control of the bad internal objects stops all truly good relationships. The individual feels dead inside and the world appears still and colorless. Finally, manic defense involves the denial of depressive feelings and use of exalted opposites (e.g., full as against empty, moving as against still, fast as against slow, light as against heavy, etc.) for reassurance. Manic defense also impacts on symbolism. Height and tallness, for instance, have phallic significance but they might also allude to manic defense in operation. Balloons often signify breasts but their lightness and playfulness might also be used as "contra-depressive symbols" (Winnicott 1935, p. 136).

The use of manic defense is typical of individuals who dread sadness and are unable to mourn. They gloss over disturbing events with astonishing ease, keep busy, avoid aloneness, are fun loving, have a large circle of friends, and are easily excitable. Many narcissistic, hypomanic, histrionic, and as-if personalities fit this picture.

In sum, the term *manic defense* denotes a person's proclivity to "deny the depressive anxiety that is inherent in emotional development, anxiety that belongs to the capacity of the individual to feel guilt, and also to acknowledge responsibility for instinctual experiences, and for the aggression in the fantasy that goes with individual experiences" (Winnicott 1935, pp. 143-144). With increasing maturity, the use of manic defense diminishes. Such lessening of its use is also discernible during the course of a well progressing intensive psychotherapy or psychoanalysis.

SUGGESTED READINGS

Klein, M. (1935). A contribution to the psychogenesis of manic-depressive states. In *Love, Guilt and Reparation and Other Works 1921-1945*, pp. 262-289. New York: Free Press, 1992.

_____ (1940). Mourning and its relation to manic-depressive states. In *Love, Guilt and Reparation and Other Works 1921-1945*, pp. 344-369. New York: Free Press, 1992.

Winnicott, D. W. (1935). The manic defence. In *Through Paediatrics to Psycho-Analysis: Collected Papers*, pp. 129-144. New York: Brunner/ Mazel, 1992.

29. What is the role of envy and defenses against envy in severe character pathology?

The experience of envy plays a very important role in severe character pathology. The work of Melanie Klein and her followers, and, more recently, that of Otto Kernberg shed light on the roots of envy in such individuals. These generally go deeper than the usual penis envy in women described by Freud, although the latter might also become condensed with the primitive sources of envy. First and foremost, however, it is important to distinguish between envy and jealousy. Klein noted that jealousy aims at the possession of the love object and the removal of a rival, whereas envy is directed at the love object itself and seeks to acquire its good characteristics. Jealousy involves whole objects and a triadic relationship. It is therefore a higher-level emotion. Envy, on the other hand, involves part objects and a dyadic relationship. It is therefore a more primitive emotion.

Klein traced the origin of envy to the earliest gratifying experiences with the mother. Besides bringing a sense of satisfaction, these experiences stir up in the child a wish to be the source of such relief and pleasure. This wish is the psychic foundation of envy. If the gratification continues unabated, then the experience of envy can be integrated with the parallel experience of mounting admiration, love, and gratitude. Any remnant envy becomes a basis of emulation of the primary object or is displaced to the father's authority. However, if the gratifying experiences with the mother are sporadic, their psychic value increases manifoldly and so does the envy of mother's capacity to satisfy. Such intense envy cannot be integrated with love; it becomes split off and pathological. Envy of this sort fuses with greed "making for a wish to exhaust the object entirely, not only in order to possess all its goodness but also to deplete the object purposefully so that it no longer contains anything enviable" (Segal 1974, p. 41). Envy fuels ambition but strong feelings of envy can also lead to despair and paralysis of effort. The fear of arousing envy in others (resulting from projection of one's own envious proclivity) might also underlie social and work inhibitions.

Three main defenses against envy are: (1) contempt and devaluation, (2) omnipotent control, and (3) narcissistic withdrawal. By *devaluation* and spoiling of the object that arouses envy, the subject seeks to diminish his estimation of the object. By exerting *omnipotent control*, such as by supervising, hiring, marrying, or somehow or other "owning" the envy-producing individual, his or her qualities are forcibly assigned to oneself. By *narcissistic withdrawal*, envy-arousing objects are shunned in reality and the pain of envy is diminished. Though evident in individuals with almost all types of severe personality disorders, the use of these mechanisms is most marked in narcissistic personalities.

Narcissistic patients envy their therapist's authenticity and capacity to help them. As a result, they either overidealize (denial by exaggeration) the therapist or tend to devalue his or her interventions and deny that they are receiving any help. They do not experience their treatment as a collaborative effort and, owing to their envy-driven devaluation, cannot carry within themselves an internal image of the therapist as a helpful and caring person. Powerful unconscious envy also underlies their vulnerability to negative therapeutic reactions, though clearly the latter have many other psychological determinants as well.

SUGGESTED READINGS

Kernberg, O. F. (1975). *Borderline Conditions and Pathological Narcissism.* New York: Jason Aronson.

Klein, M. (1957). Envy and gratitude. In *Envy and Gratitude and Other Works 1946–1963*, pp. 176–235. New York: Free Press, 1975.

Segal, H. (1974). *Introduction to the Work of Melanie Klein.* New York: Basic Books.

30. What other defenses characterize severe personality disorders?

The major defensive operations of severe personality disorders include (1) splitting, (2) projective identification, (3) the triad of maneuvers protecting the individual against envy, and (4) a set of psychological mechanisms loosely grouped under the term *manic defense*. This leaves four other defensive operations frequently seen in association with severe character pathology.

(1) *Primitive idealization*: This refers to the proclivity to see external objects as all good, in order to make certain that they can protect one against the bad objects and that they cannot be destroyed by one's own aggression or by that projected on to other objects. Primitive idealization differs from mature admiration in which there is retention of the capacity for ambivalence alongside genuine knowledge of the admired object. Primitive idealization is also distinct from reaction formation where there is at least an unconscious acknowledgment of aggression toward the object. It is rather a manifestation of a primitive protective fantasy in which there is meager knowledge and little or no concern for the admired object. Followers of religious cults, especially if they lack depth in their knowledge of the issues involved, constitute a cardinal example of those using primitive idealization. Less dramatic manifestations of it are, however, ubiquitous in borderline patients.

(2) *Primitive forms of denial*: Individuals with borderline personality organization typically display mutual denial of two affectively independent areas of consciousness. For instance, the individual might profess great love and fondness for someone at one occasion and at another berate the same person with comparable conviction. He or she might remember (or can be readily made to recall) the earlier contradictory stance but this has no affective relevance at all.

(3) *Dissociation*: This mechanism involves altered states of consciousness, autohypnosis, and amnesic repudiation of self

states. Dissociative mechanisms are seen mostly in those abused as children. Manifestations of dissociation vary greatly, ranging from minor amnesias and spells of absent-mindedness to fugue states and gross alterations of personality, such as multiple personality disorder.

(4) *Moral defense*: This mechanism was originally described by W. R. D. Fairbairn (1940) in connection with schizoid individuals. It has been further elaborated (under varying labels) by Leonard Shengold (1989) in his writings on soul murder, by Bjorn Killingmo (1989) in his paper on the technical implications of the concepts of conflict and deficit (see p. 148) and by Christopher Bollas (1992) in his elucidation of the "fascist state of mind". The origin of this defense is in the markedly abusive upbringing of children. The child takes the blame of abuse upon himself and "forgives" the perpetrator. This has two reasons: the child's egocentric perception, which precludes an awareness of others' independent motivations, and the child's attempt to preserve some hope and optimism. In other words, if it is he who is "bad," then by behaving better he can make his parents treat him better. To locate the "badness" in his parents would render the situation hopelessly unbearable.

In sum, severe personality disorders are characterized by the eight defensive operations (1) splitting, (2) projective identification, (3) defenses against envy, (4) manic defense, (5) primitive idealization, (6) primitive forms of denial, (7) moral defense, and (8) dissociation-based phenomena. It is not that "higher" forms of defenses (repression, reaction formation, rationalization, etc.) do not occur in conjunction with severe character pathology; it is only that the primitive defenses are predominant and get more readily activated.

SUGGESTED READINGS

Fairbairn, W. R. D. (1940). Schizoid factors in the personality. In *An Object Relations Theory of the Personality*, pp. 3–27. New York: Basic Books.

Shengold, L. (1989). *Soul Murder: The Effects of Childhood Abuse and Deprivation*, New Haven, CT: Yale University Press.

Bollas, C. (1992). *Being a Character: Psychoanalysis and Self Experience,* pp. 193–217. New York: Hill and Wang.

Part III

ORIGINS AND DEVELOPMENT

31. What is the role of constitutional and hereditary factors in the origins of personality and its disorders?

Personality is the ego-syntonic, stable, and reasonably predictable gestalt of maneuvers employed by the individual in order to negotiate between his inner instinctual and moral demands and his external realities. The term *personality* subsumes the concepts of *temperament* and *character*. *Temperament* refers to the composite of genetically transmitted affective, cognitive, and motor strengths, weaknesses, and idiosyncrasies of an individual. It includes factors such as adaptability to change, degree of aggression, sleep–wakefulness cycles, feeding patterns, affective responses to frustration, and preferred sensory modalities for being soothed (e.g., by singing, rocking, etc.). *Character* refers to the ego-syntonic and rationalized ways of thinking, wishing, fantasizing, and behaving derived from developmental experience with early caretakers. It includes factors such as ambitiousness, exhibitionism, envy, jealousy, capacity for sadness, generosity, inner morality, ethnic affiliation, and so forth. Personality, including both temperament and character, is necessarily a psychosomatic entity. Therefore, it is inconceivable that disorders of personality would be free of constitutional and hereditary contributions.

Such contributions occur at varying levels and in varying forms. First and foremost, the "basic core" (Weil 1970) of personality is itself an amalgam of the infant's given potentials and mother's evocative role vis-à-vis the child's identity. Second, the temperament of the child enters into an ongoing interplay with the environment. There is a "goodness of fit" (Thomas and Chess 1984) when the properties of the environment and its expectations are in accord with the child's intrinsic capacities. Such occurrence leads to a healthy outcome. A "bad fit," in contrast, sows the seeds of maladaptive personality functioning. (It should be emphasized that a "good fit" does not imply a total absence of conflict.) Third, the anatomical fact of belonging to one or the other sex has its own psychical consequences. These result in gender-based affectomotor and cognitive differences between normal male and female personalities. They also contribute to (though in ways that remains unclear) differences in the frequency with which various personality disorders occur in the two sexes. Antisocial and narcissistic personality disorders, for instance, occur more frequently in men, while histrionic and borderline personality disorders are more prevalent in women. Even when the same disorder exists in both sexes, its symptoms tend to differ somewhat, and these differences seem based upon both environmental and constitutional factors. Finally, heredity affects the incidence and phenomenology of personality disorder in the most dramatic form when there is a genetic proximity to major psychiatric disorders. Thus, genetic affinity to schizophrenia increases vulnerability to paranoid, schizoid, schizotypal personalities, and genetic affinity to major affective disorders increases vulnerability to depressive, cyclothymic and hypomanic personalities. Antisocial personality, too, seems to have at least some hereditary predisposition.

In sum, constitutional and hereditary factors play a significant and diverse role in the origin of personality and personality disorders. This is perhaps more marked in the case of severe personality disorders than in neurotic type (e.g., hysterical) personalities.

SUGGESTED READINGS

Nurenberger, J., and Berrettini, W. (in press). The genetics of antisocial personality disorder. In *Psychiatric Genetics*. London: Chatman & Hall, Ltd.

Thomas, A., and Chess, S. (1984). Genesis and evolution of behavioral disorders: from infancy to early adult life. *American Journal of Psychiatry* 141:1–9.

Weil, A. (1970). The basic core. *Psychoanalytic Study of the Child* 25:442–460. New York: International Universities Press.

32. Is schizotypal personality disorder related to schizophrenia?

Yes. Actually, schizotypal personality disorder has five types of links to schizophrenia: historical, conceptual, genetic, phenomenological, and therapeutic.

(1) *The historical connection*: The notion of a non-psychotic form of schizophrenia, which exists as a lifelong characterological oddity, was inherent in Eugen Bleuler's (1911) description of latent schizophrenia. Similar ideas were voiced by Gregory Zilboorg who described "ambulatory" schizophrenia and Paul Hoch and Philip Polatin who described "pseudo-neurotic" schizophrenia. Essentially all these descriptions were alike and portrayed a syndrome characterized by pervasive anxiety, a hidden yet discernible tendency toward autistic thinking, hypochondria, shallow social life, incapacity to settle on one job or life pursuit, an inner life suffused with hatred, and perverse sexuality. While addressing a subtype of schizophrenia and not a personality disorder, these descriptions nonetheless can be seen as the nosological precursors of the schizotypal personality disorder concept.

(2) *The conceptual connection*: The term *schizotypal* is a condensation of schizophrenia and genotype and was coined by Sandor Rado in 1953. Rado hypothesized that schizotypal individuals had essentially the same two constitutional defects that underlay schizophrenia: (i) deficiency in integrating pleasurable experiences, and (ii) a distorted awareness of the bodily self. These constitutional defects were responsible for the manifest symptoms of schizotypal personality disorder. Rado felt that such individuals were chronically at risk for a breakdown into a full-blown schizophrenia. In favorable circumstances, however, they could lead their entire lives without such fragmentation. Rado's ideas found a receptive exponent in Paul Meehl (1962) who suggested that an integrative neural deficit, "schizotaxia," is actually what is inherited in both the schizotypal personality disorder and in

schizophrenia proper. This underlying deficit accounts for the cognitive slippage, conviction of unlovability and the resultant social anxieties, pervasive ambivalence, and chronic anhedonia.

(3) *The genetic connection*: The Danish adoptive studies of Seymour Kety and colleagues confirmed the existence of a genetic linkage between schizophrenia and a characterological syndrome manifesting with atypical thinking, odd communication, tendency toward cognitive disorganization, chronic anhedonia, shallow interpersonal relations, poor sexual life, and multiple neurotic symptoms. Actually it was a careful review of Kety and Colleagues' (1975) "borderline schizophrenic" cases that formed the basis of empirical studies leading to the emergence of the *DSM-III* criteria of the schizotypal concept.

(4) *The phenomenological connection*: Although schizotypal personality disorder is not characterized by hallucinations and delusions, its symptomatology does overlap with schizophrenia in many other ways. Both conditions tend to display magical thinking, ideas of reference, social withdrawal, unusual perceptual experiences, eccentric behavior, odd speech, paranoid ideation, and inappropriate or constricted affect.

(5) *The therapeutic connection*: Antipsychotic medications used for schizophrenia can, in low dosages, also provide relief from the severe anxiety, depersonalization, and cognitive disorganization typical of schizotypal personality disorder.

In sum, schizotypal personality is related to schizophrenia in more ways than one. Indeed, it might represent what in the past used to be called *latent schizophrenia*.

SUGGESTED READINGS

Kety, S. S., Rosenthal, D., Wender, P. H., et al. (1975). Mental illness in biological and adoptive families of adopted individuals who have become schizophrenic: a preliminary report based on psychiatric interviews. In *Genetic Research in Psychiatry*, ed. R. R. Fieve, D. Rosenthal, and H. Brill, pp. 147–165. Baltimore: Johns Hopkins University Press.

Meehl, P. E. (1962). Schizotaxia, schizotypy, schizophrenia. *American Psychologist* 17:827–838.

Rado, S. (1953). Dynamics and classification of disordered behavior. *American Journal of Psychiatry* 110:406–416.

33. Are some severe personality disorders muted variants of affective disorders?

Perhaps. This view is not entirely without merit. The early literature of descriptive psychiatry, especially the writings of Emil Kraepelin and Ernest Kretschmer, firmly uphold this proposition. Indeed, as early as 1909, Kraepelin declared many characterological abnormalities to be the "fundamental states" of manic depressive illness. He believed that while some individuals with such characters developed an overt episodic form of the malady, many others "throughout the whole of life exist as peculiar forms of psychic personality without further development" (1921, p. 118). Among the subtypes of such personality disorders, Kraepelin included manic, depressive, and cyclothymic temperaments. Individuals with *manic temperament* were permanently exalted, glib, restless, distractible, and inordinately confident. They displayed subtle learning difficulties, were unable to form an overall view of their lives, felt a nagging aimlessness, lacked empathy for others, were averse to deep commitments, and were given to sexual promiscuity. In a sophisticated observation, Kraepelin noted that these inner difficulties were discernible even in the milder manic temperaments seen in gifted and socially successful personalities. Individuals with *depressive temperament* are "permanent[ly] gloomy . . . lack the right joy in work . . . take everything seriously . . . tormented by a certain feeling of guilt [and] constantly play with thoughts of suicide" (pp. 120–123). According to Kraepelin, such individuals lack self-confidence and initiative. They are sentimental, afraid of risk-taking, and given to psychosomatic illnesses. Individuals with *cyclothmic temperament* tend to oscillate between the manic and depressive extremes, displaying sustained, prominent, and frequent mood swings.

All the great turn-of-century descriptive psychiatrists (Bleuler, Kretschmer, Sheldon, Jaspers, and Schneider) continued to uphold the view that affective disorders had characterological counterparts. This was consistently reflected in British and

German psychiatric textbooks and in the *International Classification of Diseases* (*ICD-9*, 1980) of the World Health Organization. In the United States too, there was a continued, albeit half-hearted, endorsement. The reasons for this lack of enthusiasm were twofold: (1) until recently, nosological and phenomenological clarifications were not in the center arena of psychiatry in the United States, and (2) with the advent of somewhat half-hearted modern pharmacological treatments of affective disorders, there developed a tendency to enlarge the scope of affective disorders to include even their potentially characterological counterparts in the so-called Axis I domain. Little new research was therefore done regarding personality disorders related to major affective disorders.

A notable exception in this regard is Hagop Akiskal, who has undertaken a painstaking study of "soft bipolar-spectrum disorders." Though he seems somewhat ambivalent about a purely hypomanic personality, he does endorse the concept of depressive (dysthymic) and cyclothymic personality disorders. What is impressive about his work is that it brings three independent sets of data (genetic predisposition, clinical picture, and the results of certain neurophysiological tests) together to demonstrate the validity of these syndromes.

In sum, therefore, it does appear that some severe personality disorders (hypomanic, depressive, and especially cyclothymic) are variants of affective disorders. Such conceptualization is important since it has technical (e.g., trial of medications) as well as theoretical implications.

SUGGESTED READINGS

Akiskal, H. D. (1984). Characterological manifestations of affective disorders: toward a new conceptualization. *Integrative Psychiatry* 2:83–88.

Kraepelin, E. (1921). *Manic Depressive Illness and Paranoia*. Edinburgh, Scotland: E. S. Livingstone.

Kretschmer, E. (1925). *Physique and Character*. Trans. W. J. H. Sprott. New York: Harcourt Brace.

34. Is a traumatic childhood always associated with severe personality disorders?

The answer depends upon how one interprets this question. *If the question is whether a traumatic childhood necessarily results in an overt severe personality disorder, then the answer must be in the negative.* It is not infrequent to come across individuals who, despite having had much trauma during childhood, have made adequate and, at times, even superb adjustments during their adult lives. The reasons for this are complex and manifold. First, while childhood experiences (and their fantasy elaborations) do leave lasting impressions, there is a remarkable resiliency to the evolving psyche. Events and experiences during late childhood and adolescence (often involving extrafamilial identifications) working in tandem with burgeoning ego capacities can exert compensatory and corrective influences on early deficits and conflicts. Second, trauma itself is a double-edged sword. On the one hand, it results in psychic wounds, deformations of self-esteem, affect turbulence, conflicts, and pathologic formations. On the other hand, it can also provide a stimulus for ego growth, especially in the areas of perseverance, caution, self-reliance, altruism, sublimation, and creativity. Therefore, given the economic balance of its Janus-faced effect, a traumatic childhood might result in severe psychopathology or a strengthening of sectors of personality that amply compensate for the conflict-ridden areas. Finally, there are "invulnerable children" (Anthony 1974) whose outstanding constitutional strengths help them survive considerable adversities during childhood without a psychopathological outcome. In sum, it is likely but not necessary that a traumatic childhood will result in a severe personality disorder.

If, on the other hand, the question is whether individuals who as adults display severe personality disorders have necessarily had a traumatic childhood, the answer is in the affirmative. Individuals with schizotypal, schizoid, and paranoid personality disorders regularly give histories of being neglected and maltreated as children. Many of them were born unwanted and were unwelcome (often to the extent of being chronically wished dead) from the beginning of their lives. Others were repeatedly lied to, mocked, hated, and physically beaten. Individuals with histrionic ("infantile") and as-if personalities come from unstable home environments with multiple and shifting caretakers with whom no deep and sustained relationship was possible. Borderline patients, on the other hand, have had an intensely charged background that involved markedly inconsistent mothering and less than optimal paternal support. Individuals with antisocial personality disorder also have had self-absorbed, neglectful, or cruel parents. Often they come from broken homes. Even if their family of origin was intact, it was characterized by drinking and violence, few desirable role models, inconsistent disciplining patterns, and unconscious encouragement of the child's early delinquent behaviors. Even the better organized narcissistic personalities reveal traumatic childhood histories. While their specific talents were admired and indulged by the families, on the whole they were treated unempathically, coldly, and even spitefully. Having learned early on to trade their hopes of being accepted and loved for the second-rate intoxicant of admiration, they laboriously sought to hypertrophy their talents. Underneath the resulting veneer of success and acclaim (which narcissistic individuals often achieve), morose self-doubts, boredom, seething rage, nagging aimlessness, and a wistful sense of being emotionally cut off from others lie unabated. Their inner world gives testimony to their traumatic childhood.

SUGGESTED READINGS

Akhtar, S. (1992). *Broken Structures: Severe Personality Disorders and Their Treatment*. Northvale, NJ: Jason Aronson.

Anthony, E. J. (1974). The syndrome of the psychologically invulnerable child. In *The Child and His Family*, vol. 3, ed. E. J. Anthony and C. Koupernik. New York: John Wiley & Sons.

Furst, S., ed. (1967). *Psychic Trauma*. New York: Basic Books.

35. Do the mothers of borderline and narcissistic patients themselves have similar psychopathology?

Not necessarily, although some analysts do hold this view. Heinz Kohut (1977), for instance, proposes that the origin of narcissistic character pathology lies in faulty parental empathy with the growing child. He goes on to state that the mothers of narcissistic patients have a "pathogenic personality disorder" (p. 189) that impedes their mirroring capacities and reduces their empathic participation in their child's psychic growth. As a result, age-specific egocentrism and exhibitionism of the child are not tamed and channeled into further, realistic ambitions. Instead there develops an insistently attention-seeking and megalomanic grandiose self that forms the core of narcissistic personality disorder. James Masterson (1976) maintains an analogous view in regard to borderline personality disorder. He declares the mother of a borderline individual to be "clearly borderline" (p. 347) herself.

> Having been unable to separate from her own mother, she fosters continuance of the symbiotic union with her child, thus encouraging dependency to maintain her own emotional equilibrium. She is threatened by and is unable to deal with the infant's emerging individuality and therefore clings to the child to prevent separation, discouraging moves toward individuation by withdrawing her support. [pp. 37–38]

However, these views are riddled with problems. At least five objections to such conceptualization readily come to mind. (1) It does not do justice to the spectrum of experiences these patients report as having had with their mothers and fathers. (2) It implies a unifactorial and totally environmental etiology of borderline and narcissistic conditions while greatly minimizing the role of constitutional and hereditary factors in the causation of these disorders. (3) It accepts these patients' portrayal of their mothers at face value, ignoring that such recall is often, if not invariably, distorted by unconscious fantasies, defensive aims, transference wishes, and shifting affect states of the patient. (4) It omits the father's contribution to the child's growing personality and to the mother's libidinal economy and therefore her mothering capacities. (5) It fails to explain why all children raised by the same mother are not borderline or narcissistic.

How, then, to resolve this conflict? On the one hand, we have Kohut's and Masterson's views, along with the frequently heard, plaintive complaints of these patients about their mothers. On the other hand are the various heuristic pitfalls in attributing a personality disorder to these patients' mothers. One solution to this dilemma is the following. It is true that most if not all such patients have received less than "good enough" (Winnicott 1960) mothering during infancy and early childhood. However, factors other than inherent attributes of the mother's psychic organization might have resulted in such less-than-optimal mothering. This is not to say that the mother's personality plays no role, but to highlight the fact that mothering is a complex process that involves two persons (the mother and the infant) that can be significantly affected by the environment around it. Thus, factors extrinsic to the mother's person (e.g., less than optimal support from her own family, an abusive husband) and outside of her control (e.g., falling ill and needing hospitalization) can lead to compromised mothering. Factors within the child (e.g., constitutionally determined higher levels of anxiety and inconsolability, unconscious fantasy life) can also contribute to, aggravate, or make up for less than forthcoming maternal supplies. In effect, what ends up being reported years later as a less than "good enough" mother is an authentic intrapsychic construct to be sure, but it cannot be taken as a diagnostic statement regarding the mother's actual character organization.

SUGGESTED READINGS

Kohut, H. (1977). *Restoration of the Self*. New York: International Universities Press.

Masterson, J. F. (1976). *Psychotherapy of the Borderline Adult*. New York: Brunner/Mazel.

Winnicott, D. W. (1960). Ego distortion in terms of true and false self. In *The Maturational Processes and the Facilitating Environment*. pp. 140–152. New York: International Universities Press, 1965.

36. What is the role of the father in the genesis of severe character pathology?

Whereas contemporary psychoanalytic writings on severe character pathology tend to focus upon the undoubtedly significant early mother–child relationship, the fact remains that the father also plays a role in the genesis of these disorders. In order to appreciate this fully, it is important first to understand *the father's role in normal child development*. This consists of the following: (1) By being a protective, loving, and collaborative partner to the mother, the father facilitates and enhances her ability to devote herself to the child. (2) By offering himself as a relatively neutral, ego-oriented, new object during the rapprochement subphase of separation-individuation, the father provides the child with stability, a haven from conflict, and (in the case of a boy) an important measure of "dis-identification" (Greenson 1968) from the mother. (3) By appearing on the evolving psychic horizon of the child as the romantic partner of the mother, the father helps consolidate the child's capacity to experience, bear, and benefit from the triangular familial relationship and the conflicts attendant upon it. (4) By presenting himself as an admirable model for identification to his son and by reflecting the budding femininity of his daughter with restrained reciprocity, the father enriches his children's gender identity and gives direction to their later sexual object choices. All this results in a powerful impact on both the ego and superego, especially in the realm of disengagement from mother, language organization, modulation of aggression, establishment of incest barrier, acceptance of generational boundaries, capacity to respect and idealize elders, entry into the temporal order, and, through it, a deeper sense of familial and ethnic affiliation.

It is not surprising, therefore, that *the weakness or absence or the intrusiveness and sadism of the father contribute heavily to the potential of severe character pathology in the offspring*. Overt sexual and/or physical abuse by the father are obviously injurious to the growing child's psyche. However, the problematic aspects of the father's role are usually more subtle. During preoedipal development, the father's lack of love and support for the mother has deleterious effects upon the mother–infant relation through the mother's psychic reality. This could result in a weakness of mother–child attachment or the mother's anxious clinging to her child to compensate for the deficient libidinal supplies from her mate. A father who is weak or absent (physically or psychologically) also fails to disengage the child from the mother's symbiotic orbit. This tends to perpetuate the child's wish/fear of fusion with the mother and lays the groundwork for lifelong struggles over dependence and autonomy that are characteristic of all severe personality disorders. Still later in childhood, a denigrated father (especially in combination with an overindulgent mother) deprives the boy of a true oedipal experience, with the resulting clinical picture of irreverent bravado, cockiness, and promiscuity on the one hand and intense castration anxiety, unconscious guilt, self-destructiveness, and lifelong father hunger on the other hand. This phenomenology is frequent in male narcissistic personalities. In the girl's case, an overindulgent father (especially in combination with a depressed and emotionally unavailable mother) imparts not only the aforementioned oedipal triumph constellation to her but also robs her of the basic prototype of mourning (loss of the "all good" mother) thus fixating her in the pathological hope of reversing the preoedipal trauma by external means.

SUGGESTED READINGS

Chasseguet-Smirgel, J. (1984). *Creativity and Perversion*. New York: Norton.
Greenson, R. (1968). Dis-identifying from mother: its special importance for the boy. *International Journal of Psycho-Analysis* 49:370–374.
Rothstein, A. (1979). Oedipal conflicts in narcissistic personality disorders. *International Journal of Psycho-Analysis* 60:189–199.

37. Do patients with severe personality disorders have oedipal problems also?

Yes. While their problems are mainly of preoedipal origin, the fact remains that in clinical practice oedipal and preoedipal issues cannot be surgically separated. Developmentally also, the two have a reciprocal influence upon each other. *The preoedipal phase invariably affects and sometimes even determines the shape of the Oedipus complex.* For instance, a profound lack of libidinal ministrations by the mother, perhaps going as far back as the symbiotic phase, might result in a tragic lack of activation of early eroticism. Such neglect, if continued over the later part of infancy and childhood, may preclude a substantial enough oedipal experience from occurring. This seems to be the case in profoundly sadomasochistic schizoid and paranoid characters who show an obliteration of gender markers and a life style altogether devoid of tenderness, romance, and sexuality. Such structural thinness of the oedipal experience is also evident in profoundly infantile and as-if characters with a background of unstable, shifting, and multiple caretakers during the first few years of life. These individuals lack the capacity for mature love, do not truly understand the incest barrier, and can readily trade one love object for another. Narcissistic and borderline individuals, in contrast, often give evidence of a precocious and extraordinarily intense Oedipus complex. In both these characterological formations, there is a condensation of oedipal and preoedipal conflicts under the overriding influence of pregenital, especially oral, aggression (Kernberg 1975). The orally tinged craving for the "all-good" mother intensifies the oedipal longing, while the projection of oral rage establishes exaggerated castration fears in the mind. Among the various phenomenological outcomes is sexual promiscuity, to obtain oral supplies through oedipal aims, and homosexuality, to renounce oedipal competition altogether. More often, one sees poorly object-related, desperate heterosexuality covering up a tenuous and fluctuating sexual orientation in borderline and narcissistic patients. In 1977, Kernberg highlighted the *constellations of preoedipally distorted oedipal conflicts in borderline patients.* These include (1) an excessively aggressive coloring of oedipal conflicts, (2) an undue idealization of the heterosexual love object in the positive oedipal relation and of the homosexual love object in the negative oedipal relation, (3) a highly unrealistic quality to the fantasied relations with either of these objects, (4) a pregenital agenda to seemingly genital strivings, and (5) a premature oedipalization of preoedipal conflicts. While these characteristics are reflected in the borderline individual's sexual behavior, fantasies, and interpersonal relations, their value for diagnostic purposes is less than that of the psycho-structural and defensive characteristics of these patients.

Among male narcissistic patients, one sometimes comes across a peculiarly split oedipal configuration, with an attitude of oedipal triumph (often facilitated by an overindulgent mother and a weak father) on the one hand, and terrifying castrating anxiety on the other. The resulting clinical picture comprises, on the one hand, irreverence, undue bravado, sexual promiscuity, an inability to respect the institution of marriage, and an atemporal life style with little regard for generational differences, and, on the other hand, secret and intense fear of authority, bouts of sexual impotence, doubts regarding physical integrity and prowess, feeling like a little boy, a lifelong hunger for an admirable father, and unconscious seeking of punishment for one's transgressions.

SUGGESTED READINGS

Kernberg, O. F. (1975). *Borderline Conditions and Pathological Narcissism*, pp. 40–44. New York: Jason Aronson.
_____ (1977). The structural diagnosis of borderline personality organization. In *Borderline Personality Disorders: the Concept, the Syndrome, the Patient*, ed. P. Hartocollis, pp. 87–121. New York: International Universities Press.
Rothstein, C. (1979). Oedipal conflicts in narcissistic personality disorders. *International Journal of Psycho-Analysis* 60:189–199.

38. How can one distinguish between preoedipal and oedipal pathology?

In any attempt at distinguishing between preoedipal and oedipal pathology, one should keep in mind that *there is no such thing as purely preoedipal or purely oedipal pathology.* The two themes invariably coexist. They might be condensed into each other or one might serve as a defense against the emergence of the other. Oedipal wishes are often associated with preoedipal (e.g., separation) fears, and preoedipal object hunger frequently takes on a triangular and sexualized coloring. Oedipal drive derivatives can camouflage unresolved symbiotic longings, and a preoedipal baby-like pleading can be a regressive refuge from the guilt and anxiety provoking oedipal competitiveness.

Manifest symptomatology, therefore, is not a good enough guide to distinguish between preoedipal and oedipal pathology. More helpful is to discern whether libidinal object constancy (Mahler et al. 1975) has been achieved and whether a coherent sense of his or her identity exists in the individual. A broad-based assessment of the developmental level of the patient is therefore necessary. *Greenspan (1977) has outlined seven areas of personality functioning that should be scrutinized during such an assessment* including:

(1) capacity for distinguishing internal v. external reality; (2) cohesion, organization and resistance to fragmentation even under stress of the self and object representations; (3) capacity for experiencing and perceiving a variety of discriminated affect states; (4) level of defences; (5) capacity to modulate impulses appropriate to external situation; (6) capacity for genuine attachment and separation, and for the experience of sadness and mourning; and (7) capacity for integration of love and hate (fusion of good and bad, aggression and libido). [p. 385]

Individuals whose characters are predominantly organized around preoedipal levels carry an intense emotional conviction about the reality of their "fantasies." They might superficially acknowledge them as fantasies but are deeply reluctant to modify their ideas. Such individuals also display a fragility of self- and object representations. They tend to stubbornly maintain a particular view of themselves or the therapist, failing to see either in any other way. Their affects are limited though intense. They show a predominance of primitive ego defenses (e.g., splitting, denial, projective identification) and have difficulty with impulse control. They cannot synthesize polarities and think in "either-or" terms (e.g., your way or my way, now or never, all or none, love or hate, good or bad). They also lack the capacity for mournful sadness. This should not be surprising since these individuals have not had a successful separation-individuation and thus lack the prototype of sadness that comes from truly letting go of the early dyadic partner ("the mother of symbiosis").

In addition, a preoedipal personality organization is characterized by the predominance of object relations conflicts, whereas the oedipal organization is characterized by structural conflicts. In

> a structural conflict, the subject experiences (or is capable of experiencing if some part of the conflict is unconscious) the opposing tendencies as aspects of himself. . . . In the object relations conflict, the subject experiences the conflict as being between his own wishes and his representations (e.g., introjects) of another person's values, prohibitions, or injunctions. [Dorpat 1976, pp. 869–870]

SUGGESTED READINGS

Dorpat, T. L. (1976). Structural conflict and object relations conflict. *Journal of the American Psychoanalytic Association* 24:855–874.

Greenspan, S. I. (1977). The oedipal-preoedipal dilemma: a reformulation in the light of object relations theory. *International Review of Psycho-Analysis* 6:612–627.

Mahler, M. S., Pine, F., and Bergman, A. (1975). *The Psychological Birth of the Human Infant*. New York: Basic Books.

39. What are Fairbairn's contributions to the understanding of schizoid character?

More than any other investigator, W. R. D. Fairbairn, an early Scottish psychoanalyst, delved into the phenomenology and dynamics of the schizoid condition. In his psychoanalytic work with schizoid patients, Fairbairn (1940) found that

(1) in early life they gained the conviction, whether through apparent indifference or through apparent possessiveness on the part of their mother, that their mother did not really love and value them as persons in their own right; (2) influenced by a resultant sense of deprivation and inferiority, they remained profoundly fixated upon their mother; (3) the libidinal attitude accompanying this fixation was one not only characterized by extreme dependence, but also rendered highly self preservative and narcissistic by anxiety over a situation which presented itself as involving a threat to the ego; (4) through a regression to the attitude of the early oral phase, not only did the libidinal cathexis of an already internalized "breast-mother" become internalized, but also the process of internalization itself became unduly extended to relationship with other objects; and (5) these resulted in general overvaluation of the internal at the expense of the external world. [p. 23]

Fairbairn elaborated on the phenomenological consequences of such a fixation. The regressive substitution of mother as a person by a more easily controllable part object, the breast, led in such individuals to an overall tendency to treat other people as less than persons with an inherent value of their own. This powerful tendency toward a simplification of relationships often resulted in their substituting bodily for emotional contacts. The persistence of this early attitude also manifested in the predominance of taking over giving in the emotional life. Fairbairn pointed out that schizoid individuals feel exhausted after social contacts and defend against their difficulty in emotional giving by playing roles that replace giving by showing.

Fairbairn observed that the attraction of artistic and literary activities for schizoid individuals is partly due to the fact that these activities provide an exhibitionistic means of expression without involving direct contact. However, he pointed out that schizoid individuals have another reason for keeping their love to themselves. They fear that the vigor of their needs can deplete others and therefore come to regard loving as dangerous. To hide their love and to protect themselves from others' love, rendered dangerous by projection, schizoid individuals erect defenses against loving and being loved. They feel compelled to distance others by seeming indifferent or by being rude, even hateful. According to Fairbairn, this substitution of loving by hating has two motives, one immoral, the other moral:

> The immoral motive is determined by the consideration that, since the joy of loving seems hopelessly barred to him, he may as well deliver himself over to the joy of hating and obtain what satisfaction he can out of that. . . . The moral motive is determined by the consideration that, if loving involves destroying, it is better to destroy by hate, which is overtly destructive and bad, than to destroy by love, which is by rights creative and good. [p. 27]

Fairbairn thus viewed schizoid individuals as suffering from three tragedies. The first is that they feel that their love is destructive. The second is that they exhibit a defensive compulsion to hate and be hated while longing deep down to be loved. The third is that the situation thus necessitates an "amazing reversal of moral values" (p. 27) portraying love to be an inferior and more dangerous emotion than hate.

SUGGESTED READINGS

Fairbairn, W. R. D. (1940). Schizoid factors in the personality. In *An Object Relations Theory of the Personality*, pp. 3–27. New York: Basic Books.

Guntrip, H. (1969). *Schizoid Phenomena, Object Relations and the Self*, pp. 17–48. New York: International Universities Press.

Sutherland, J. D. (1989). *Fairbairn's Journey into the Interior*. London: Free Association Books.

40. What are Winnicott's views on the *antisocial tendency*?

In a paper of remarkable theoretical and technical significance, Donald Winnicott (1956) presented his views on the *antisocial tendency*. Although his clinical descriptions involved children, Winnicott stated that manifestations of antisocial tendency could be seen in individuals of all ages. He emphasized that antisocial tendency did not constitute a diagnosis. Such phenomena could occur in association with character disorders, psychotic, neurotic, and even nearly normal mental states.

Winnicott used the designation *antisocial tendency* for those attitudes and actions of an individual that compel the environment to be important. It is as if the individual, by behaving in a certain manner, forces the environment to attend to him. Viewed in this manner, antisocial tendency is a desperate manifestation of the hope that someone will listen and do something to change the situation. Winnicott went on to state that stealing and destructiveness are always present in the antisocial tendency, though one or the other might be more marked in a given case.

> By *one* trend the child is looking for something, somewhere, and failing to find it seeks elsewhere, when hopeful. By the *other* the child is seeking that amount of environmental stability which will stand the strain resulting from impulsive behavior. This is a search for an environmental provision that has been lost. [p. 310, Winnicott's italics]

The individual who steals is not looking for the stolen object but is seeking a person over whom he could have such unlimited rights. Similarly, destructiveness is aimed at hurting someone with an underlying hope of being accepted by that person. This "nuisance value" (p. 311) is an essential aspect of the antisocial tendency that seeks repeatedly to test the environment's containing capacity and resilience. Its manifestations include imperiousness, greediness, messiness, stealing, lying, outrageousness, and overt destructiveness.

Winnicott traced the origin of the antisocial tendency to a traumatic experience of deprivation in childhood. There has been

> a loss of something good that has been positive in the child's experience up to a certain date, and that has been withdrawn; the withdrawal has extended over a period of time longer than that over which the child can keep the memory of the experience alive. [p. 309, Winnicott's italics]

It is this rupture of homeostasis that the individual behaving in an antisocial manner is seeking to repair. There is, therefore, a self-curative element in such behavior.

Winnicott explicitly stated that the treatment of the antisocial tendency is not psychoanalysis but "management, tolerance, and understanding . . . a going to meet and match the moment of hope" (p. 309). The therapist, representing the environment, must offer a new opportunity for ego relatedness since it was an environmental failure in ego support that originally led to the antisocial tendency. While Winnicott does not say so, his view of the antisocial tendency has considerable impact on one's interpretive stance vis-à-vis a patient's acting out. For instance, a patient's intrusions on the therapist's personal life, instead of being viewed as undesirable translation of prohibited unconscious wishes into action, might be seen as the expression of an understandable need to have someone from whose space one would not be excluded. Clearly the two stances lead to different therapeutic strategies. These should not be viewed as mutually exclusive and a psychotherapeutic or psycho-analytic technique accommodating both perspectives (Akhtar 1992, Strenger 1989) should be developed.

SUGGESTED READINGS

Akhtar, S. (1992). *Broken Structures: Severe Personality Disorders and Their Treatment*, pp. 316–324. Northvale, NJ: Jason Aronson.

Strenger, C. (1989). The classic and the romantic visions of psychoanalysis. *International Journal of Psycho-Analysis* 70:595–610.

Winnicott, D. W. (1956). The antisocial tendency. In *Through Paediatrics to Psychoanalysis*, pp. 306–315. London: Tavistock, 1958.

41. What is meant by *cumulative trauma*?

The term *cumulative trauma* was introduced into psychoanalytic literature by Masud Khan in 1963. While Ernst Kris (1956) had earlier mentioned a similar concept under the rubric of *strain trauma*, it was Khan who became the leading exponent of this very significant idea. According to him, "cumulative trauma is the result of the breaches in the mother's role as a protective shield over the whole course of the child's development, from infancy to adolescence — that is to say, in all those areas of experience where the child continues to need the mother as an auxiliary ego to support his immature and unstable ego functions" (1963, p. 46). These breaches in the mother's role as a protective shield are not singly traumatic. However, their effect accumulates silently and becomes traumatic, as it were, in retrospect.

Khan acknowledged that even under normal circumstances there are occasional failures in the mother's function as a protective shield, a function that defends the infant/child from unmanageable excitations from outside and unbearable instinctual tensions from within. However, such failures are temporary and readily mitigated by the mother's subsequent empathic attunement. It is when failures of the mother in her role as a protective shield are quite frequent that they begin to set up a nucleus of pathogenic reactions. The resulting interplay between the mother and infant can have any or all of the following effects: (1) There occurs a *premature and selective ego development*. Some of the emerging autonomous functions of the ego become accelerated in growth and begin to serve defensive functions against unpleasurable impingements with which the child cannot otherwise deal. There might also develop "a special responsiveness in the infant-child to the mother's mood that creates an imbalance in the integration of aggressive drives" (Khan 1964, pp. 62–63). As adults, such individuals might display a chameleon-like adaptability to their environments. Inwardly, they feel that they are mere responders to others' cues and not initiators with their own will. (2) The involvement of precocious ego development with the mother's collusive response leads to *impaired differentiation into a self-unit* and deficient personalization. Instead of a coherent and autonomous self, there develop multiple dissociations within the self. "A characteristic of this type of dissociated ego-development is that what should have been a silent, unregistered dependency state changes into a coercive militant and engineered exploitation of instinctual and ego dependence" (1964, p. 63). (3) There develops a *hypercathexis of both internal and external reality* as well as an undue need to remain stimulated. Such individuals crave activity and excitement. They cannot be peacefully alone and inactive. Their hyper-reflectiveness about themselves and their relentless need to be tantalized serve as defenses against inner emptiness, apathy, and nonexistence.

Cumulative trauma builds up silently throughout childhood and its disruptive effects become manifest largely at adolescence. Then the collusive mother–child bond is vehemently rejected, leading to willful negativism, inertia, futility and depression or, in a flight from such painful affects, a passionate search for new ideals and objects. In the clinical setting, effects of cumulative trauma lead to archaic affectivity, intense sensitivity to the therapist's interventions and silences, and a marked propensity for enactments on the patient's part. The therapist, on the other hand, has to be vigilant about his countertransference. It is only through a disciplined screening of his own affects and impulses that the therapist can avoid trying to become a "better mother" for the patient while offering himself as an auxiliary ego that performs both containing and interpretive functions.

SUGGESTED READINGS

Khan, M. M. R. (1963). The concept of cumulative trauma. In *The Privacy of the Self*, pp. 42–58. New York: International Universities Press, 1974.
_____ (1964). Ego distortion, cumulative trauma and the role of reconstruction in the analytic situation. In *The Privacy of the Self*, pp. 59–68. New York: International Universities Press, 1974.
Kris, E. (1956). The recovery of childhood memories in psychoanalysis. *Psychoanalytic Study of the Child* 11:54–88. New York: International Universities Press.

42. What does Mahler's theory of separation-individuation essentially propose?

The most fundamental proposition of Margaret Mahler's symbiosis and separation-individuation theory is that the psychological birth of the human infant, that is, the beginning in the child of a coherent sense of personhood, is distinct from its biological birth. Based upon extensive observational studies, Mahler postulated a sequence of developmental and maturational events through which a child must pass before becoming separate enough from the mother and acquiring a fairly stable sense of being a unique entity. The first such phase is the *autistic phase* in which the neonate is self-contained and encased as if by a psychophysiological stimulus barrier. There is, however, increasing question as to the existence of this phase in the light of recent infant observational research. Next is the *symbiotic phase* in which a dual unity exists between the mother and the infant, and the "basic core" (Weil 1970) of the infant's self awakens in a state of enmeshment with the mother's self. This is followed by the *separation-individuation phase*, which has four subphases. First among these is the *differentiation subphase* (from about 4–5 to 8–9 months) in which the child starts to learn about his psychological separateness through rudimentary explorations of the self as well as the mother's environment. Next is the *practicing subphase* (from 9 to 16–18 months) in which the toddler elatedly enjoys his newfound psychomotor autonomy and appears to be involved in the "conquest of the world." Then comes the *rapprochement subphase* (from about 16 to about 24 months) in which the child learns that his separateness, autonomy, and motor abilities have their limits. The realities of the external world appear harsh and the child regresses in the hope of reestablishing the lost symbiotic bliss with the mother. This return, however, is ambivalent, since the drive of individuation is at work with greater force. The resulting "ambitendency" accounts for the alternating cycles of dependence and flight characteristic of a child in this phase. If overcome, the rapprochement phase is followed by a period designated *on the road to object constancy*, in which a deeper, somewhat ambivalent, but more sustained object representation is internalized, the libidinal attachment to which does not become seriously compromised by temporary frustrations. This is accompanied by a more realistic and less shifting view of the self. The attainment of object constancy assures the mother's lasting presence in the child's mental structure. The attainment of self constancy establishes a coherent, single self-representation with minimal fluctuations under drive pressures.

Mahler emphasized that two conditions must be met for organization of the ego and neutralization of drives to arrive at a sense of identity: (1) the enteroceptive-proprioceptive stimuli must not be so continual and so intense as to prevent structure formation; thus a shift from viscera-centered splanchnic innervation to the external rind of body ego is essential for self boundary formation, and (2) the mother must be able to buffer and organize inner and other stimuli for the infant. The libidinal ministrations of the mother during the symbiotic phase and the aggressive hurts and bumps during the practicing phase both constitute the outlines, as it were, of the child's bodily self-awareness. However, it is not until the end of the rapprochement subphase of separation-individuation, an event occurring at approximately 2 years of age, that a stable sense of one's unique and separate personhood comes into being. The renewed clinging as well as the valiant self-assertion of the toddler during this phase must be met with a constant but empathic stance from the mother. Internalization of this maternal attitude permits the needy and the omnipotent self-images of the child to unite and form a realistic view of the self.

SUGGESTED READINGS

Mahler, M. S. (1968). *On Human Symbiosis and the Vicissitudes of Individuation*. New York: International Universities Press.

Mahler, M. S., Pine, F., and Bergman, A. (1975). *The Psychological Birth of the Human Infant*. New York: Basic Books.

Weil, A. (1970). The basic core. *Psychoanalytic Study of the Child* 25:442–460. New York: International Universities Press.

43. What are the consequences of impaired object constancy?

As early as 1971, Mahler noted that a failure to develop object constancy is associated with clinical signs that indicate

> that the blending and synthesis of "good" and "bad" self-and object image have not been achieved; that ego-filtered affects have become inundated by surplus unneutralized aggression; that delusions of omnipotence alternate with utter dependency and self-denigration; that the body image has become or remains suffused with unneutralized id-related erogeneity and aggressive, pent-up body feeling, and so on. [p. 181]

All this translates into the following six clinical manifestations:

(1) *Disturbances of optimal distance*: The failure to achieve object constancy leads to difficulty in maintaining optimal distance. Involvement with others stirs up a dilemma: to be intimate is to risk engulfment and to be apart is to court loneliness. In an attempt to solve this dilemma, the borderline continues to go back and forth. The narcissist sustains allegiances longer and shows slower oscillations in relationships. The paranoid bristles at any change in distance initiated by others, preferring the reliability of his fear of being betrayed. The schizoid withdraws on the surface but maintains an intense imaginary tie to his objects. The antisocial and the hypomanic, though inwardly uncommitted, rapidly develop superficial intimacy with others. Disturbances of optimal distance also manifest in certain chronic marital difficulties in which the partners can neither live with nor without each other.

(2) *Splitting and intensification of affects*: Another result of failed object constancy is the persistence of split self-and object representations. Splitting leads to repeated, intense, and convincing oscillations of self-esteem, intolerance of ambivalence, and a tendency to react to realistic setbacks with negative mood swings. In persons with action-prone egos, such flooding with unneutralized aggression might result in destructive and violent acts.

(3) *Paranoid tendencies*: As a reciprocal of libidinal object constancy, some individuals cling to an "inconstant object" (Blum 1981). They constantly fear being betrayed by it but cannot permit it its own existence. This is a desperate effort to preserve an illusory constant object even though tinged with aggression.

(4) *Inordinate optimism and the "someday" fantasy*: The continued inner clinging to the "all good" mother of symbiosis fuels the hope of "someday" finding such an object in external reality. This underlies the frantic search of the borderline, the steadfast ambition of the narcissist, the gambling nature of the antisocial, and the passive waiting stance of the schizoid.

(5) *Malignant erotic transference*: When the pursuit of the "all good" mother of symbiosis becomes condensed with positive oedipal strivings, it gives rise to a very intense, coercive, regressive, destructive, and inconsolable erotic transference.

(6) *Inability to mourn, nostalgia, and the "if only" fantasy*: The pressure to recapture the pre-separation, symbiotic bond with the mother impairs the mourning capacity and underlies the "if only" fantasy. Individuals with such a fantasy keep wringing their hands over some past occurrence. They insist that "if only" it had not occurred, everything would have turned out all right. Life before that event is retrospectively idealized, with a consequent vulnerability to intense nostalgia.

In sum, lack of object constancy impairs the capacities to mourn, tolerate ambivalence, and maintain optimal distance. Lacking inner cohesion, such individuals tend to develop compensatory structures leading to paranoia, erotomania, and inconsolable nostalgia.

SUGGESTED READINGS

Akhtar, S. (1994). Object constancy and adult psychopathology. *International Journal of Psycho-Analysis* 75:441–455.

Blum, H. (1981). Object inconstancy and paranoid conspiracy. *Journal of the American Psychoanalytic Association* 29:789–813.

Mahler, M. S. (1971). A study of the separation-individuation process and its possible application to borderline phenomena in the psychoanalytic situation. *Psychoanalytic Study of the Child* 26:402–424. New Haven, CT: Yale University Press.

44. What are Kernberg's views on the genesis of borderline personality organization?

In his seminal paper, "Borderline Personality Organization," Kernberg (1967) proposed that for a coherent structuring of the self and for the internalization of object relationships, the early ego has to accomplish two tasks. *The first task involves the differentiation of self images from object images which form part of early introjections and identifications.* In order for this task to be accomplished, the autonomous ego functions should be intact and maturing at an expected pace. Moreover, there should be regular and predictable gratification of instinctual needs to make the distinction between self and non-self tolerable. A moderate amount of instinctual frustration also helps because it brings to awareness the painful absence of the gratifying object and thus demarcates the self from the object. Constitutional vulnerabilities of the autonomous ego functions, excessive gratification, and excessive frustration all tend to reinforce the normal disposition to regressive loss of self-object disorientation, that is, the failure of the first task. This is characteristic of a psychotic level of organization.

The second task is that self- and object representations built under the influence of libidinal drive derivatives and their corresponding affects have to be integrated with self- and object representations built under the influence of aggressive drive derivatives and their corresponding affects. In other words, idealized "all good" images of the objects have to be integrated with their devalued "all bad" images, and the exalted self-views have to be tempered by inferiority-laden self-views. As a result of this synthesis, somewhat ambivalent albeit deeper and richer views of the self and the objects emerge. Self- and object representations become further differentiated from each other and also more realistic. However, in order for this task to be accomplished, two things are required. One is that the memory apparatuses, associated with the autonomous ego functions, mature to the extent that contradictory self- and object representations can actually be kept simultaneously in mind and not merely forgotten. Second, the intensity of aggressive drive derivatives should not be so overwhelming as to totally eclipse the loving self- and object representations and thus impede the mending of the split between the two sets of self- and object representations. Such "excessive aggression may stem both from a constitutionally determined intensity of aggressive drives or from severe early frustration" (Kernberg 1967, p. 666).

The failure of this second task, that is, integration of aggressive and libidinal self- and object representations, characterizes the borderline personality organization. The lack of synthesis results in the persistence of splitting as the main defensive operation of the ego. Primitive, unrealistic, and contradictory self-representations continue to exist and are readily activated by environmental cues. Contradictory object representations cannot be integrated either. Consequently, the world appears to be populated by "gods" and "devils," but no true human beings. Associated with all this is a characteristic intensification of affect, impairment of decision-making processes, and, most importantly, the syndrome of identity diffusion. Such a pathological state of affairs precludes a satisfactory oedipal experience. The preoedipal pathology distorts the Oedipus complex and the resulting clinical picture displays the condensation of those two under the dominance of pregenital aggression.

SUGGESTED READINGS

Akhtar S., and Byrne, J. P. (1983). The concept of splitting and its clinical relevance. *American Journal of Psychiatry* 140:1013–1016.

Kernberg, O. F. (1967). Borderline personality organization. *Journal of the American Psychoanalytic Association* 15:641–685.

_____ (1977). The structural diagnosis of borderline personality organization. In *Borderline Personality Disorders: the Concept, the Syndrome, the Patient*, ed. P. Hartocollis, pp. 87–121. New York: International Universities Press.

45. How do Kernberg's and Kohut's views on narcissistic personality differ?

Otto Kernberg and Heinz Kohut differ in their conceptualization of narcissistic personality disorder. Their differences can be grouped under three categories: (1) phenomenology, (2) pathogenesis and metapsychology, and (3) treatment technique.

(1) *Phenomenology:* Kernberg's description of narcissistic personality differs from that of Kohut in four ways. First, he emphasizes the paranoid substrate of the syndrome and hence regards mistrust, hunger, rage, and guilt about this rage to be the basic cause of the self-inflation and not merely reactive phenomena, as Kohut proposes. Second, he gives a special place to the chronic envy that underlies the narcissistic person's seeming scorn for others. Indeed, Kernberg considers defenses against such envy, particularly devaluation, omnipotent control, and narcissistic withdrawal, a major aspect of the clinical picture of narcissistic personality disorder. Third, while Kohut considers spontaneously unfolding transferences to be the only reliable tool in diagnosis, Kernberg (in his usual attitude of rapprochement with general psychiatry), provides detailed behavioral criteria for the diagnosis of narcissistic personality. Kernberg then differentiates it from other personality disorders, including borderline and antisocial personalities on one hand and obsessional and hysterical personalities on the other. Finally, unlike Kohut, Kernberg does not attribute the middle-aged narcissist's denial of his age-specific limitations and his envy of younger generations to a failure in achieving his true destiny. Instead, he suggests that the deterioration of the narcissist's internal world is yet another step in the repeating cycles of desire, idealization, greedy incorporation, and disappearance of supplies by spoiling, disappointing, and devaluation.

(2) *Pathogenesis and metapsychology*: Here the differences between Kohut's and Kernberg's views involve: (1) narcissism's

separateness versus necessary relationship with object relations, (2) a developmental arrest versus a pathological formation view of the grandiose self, (3) the reactive versus the fundamental substrate view of aggression, and (4) the relative importance of the Oedipus complex in pathological narcissism. Kohut sees the etiology of the disorder in parental empathic failure, leading to a developmental arrest upon archaic forms of grandiosity and self-esteem regulation. Kernberg regards such pathological grandiosity to have developed as a defense against paranoid anxieties consequent to splitting and projection of aggressive self- and object-representations with secondary distortions of the Oedipus complex.

(3) *Treatment technique*: Kohut emphasizes the reparative function of the analyst in the psychoanalytic treatment of narcissistic personality; Kernberg steadfastly underscores the interpretative function of the analyst. Kohut emphasizes empathy as a therapeutic tool; Kernberg regards it as a technical necessity for interpretation. Kohut makes reductionistic, linear reconstructions of childhood traumata from patients' conscious recall; Kernberg posits that narcissistic transferences at first activate past defenses against deeper relationships with parents and only then the real past relationships. When rage appears in treatment, Kohut views it as reactive to empathic failures of the analyst that reactivate similarly traumatizing experiences from the past; Kernberg views pregenital aggression as the basic, inciting agent against which the grandiose self is built as a defense. His suggested technique insists upon a thorough interpretation of negative transference developments in their defensive as well as recapitulation aspects.

SUGGESTED READINGS

Akhtar, S. (1989). Kohut and Kernberg: a critical comparison. In *Self Psychology: Comparisons and Contrasts*, eds. D. W. Detrick and S. P. Detrick, pp. 329–362. Hillsdale, NJ: Analytic Press.

Kernberg, O. F. (1975). *Borderline Conditions and Pathological Narcissism*, pp. 227–314. New York: Jason Aronson.

Kohut, H. (1977). *The Restoration of the Self*. New York: International Universities Press.

Part IV

EVALUATION
AND TRIAGE

46. How does a psychodynamic interview differ from conventional medical history taking?

Psychodynamic interviewing differs from conventional history taking in important ways. Glen Gabbard (1990) has astutely outlined five major differences among them.

(1) In customary medical interviewing, physicians pursue a direct and linear course. Patients are eager to be helped and therefore cooperate with the interviewer. In psychiatry, however, such a process does not work well. Patients are themselves unclear, ambivalently motivated, resistant, and often embarrassed about their problems. They may defensively exaggerate certain aspects of their problems while consciously or unconsciously minimizing other aspects. The interview process is therefore not solely and narrowly focused upon fact gathering but upon the ebb and flow of the process itself since these reveal important information about the patient.

(2) In medical interviewing, it is clear that establishing a diagnosis precedes treatment. In dynamic interviewing, one approaches the patient with the understanding that the manner of the diagnostic interview might itself contain therapeutic elements. Instances in which a recommendation of "no treatment" is made after the evaluation are actually instances of recommending "no further treatment" because the evaluation has itself been therapeutic enough.

(3) Another difference between medical and psychodynamic interviewing lies in the dimension of activity and passivity. Patients are usually passive participants in the former setting. In the latter, however, the clinician actively engages the patient as a collaborator in an exploratory process. He regards the patient as potentially capable of contributing a great deal to the diagnostic understanding that will evolve from the initial evaluation.

(4) Yet another distinction between traditionally medical and psychodynamic orientation in clinical interviewing pertains to the

selection of relevant data. In the former setting, eliciting symptom constellations for arriving at a syndromal diagnosis is the main concern. Psychodynamic interviewing, in contrast, is interested in more than a symptomatic diagnosis. It is geared toward a deeper understanding of the patient's intrapsychic world and his life as a person. Sectors of mind in which healthy functioning has indeed been achieved, sublimations, talents, and evidences of perseverance, honesty, verbal facility, and wit are of as much interest to the dynamic interviewer as are the areas of conflict, suffering, and doubt. This is because understanding of the patient's personality can come from healthy as well as unhealthy areas. Moreover, the elucidation of the former is also important for making therapeutic plans and prognostic assessments.

(5) Finally, a unique aspect of dynamic interviewing is the emphasis on the clinician's feelings during the process. In customary history taking, subjective emotions of the clinician are regarded as obstacles to a task. In dynamic interviewing, however, such feelings are themselves a source of information about the patient. They inform the clinician of what the patient characteristically stirs up in others, and hence give a valuable clue to his intrapsychic and interpersonal life.

In sum, dynamic interviewing is a much more complex, affectively rich, and interactive process than the customary checklist sort of history taking. The information it yields about the patient is more meaningful and more extensive.

SUGGESTED READINGS

Gabbard, G. (1990). *Psychodynamic Psychiatry in Clinical Practice*. Washington, DC: American Psychiatric Press.

Mackinnon, R. A., and Michels, R. (1971). *The Psychiatric Interview in Clinical Practice*. Philadelphia: W. B. Saunders.

Shevrin, H., and Schectman, F. (1973). The diagnostic process in psychiatric evaluations. *Bulletin of the Menninger Clinic* 37:451–494.

47. What are the various steps in the initial evaluation process?

A thorough initial evaluation usually takes two to three sessions and consists of *six tasks*. These are: (1) responding to the first telephone call from the patient and setting up an appointment; (2) observing the patient's appearance and overall behavior, including his manner of arrival for the appointment; (3) gathering information about the patient's symptomatology, identity consolidation, object relations, and developmental history; (4) establishing and protecting a therapeutic framework; (5) assessing the patient's psychological-mindedness; and (6) sharing the diagnostic conclusions and making treatment recommendations. (Only the first two of these six tasks will be addressed here. The other tasks will be taken up individually in subsequent sections.)

(1) *Responding to the first phone call*: The first contact between a patient and his or her therapist usually occurs via telephone. This is an important aspect of the initial encounter and can provide valuable information besides being the first step in establishing a therapeutic framework. First of all, therefore, one should return a phone call from a potential patient only when one has some peaceful and uninterrupted time available. While lengthy conversation at this point is generally inadvisable, having the cushion of a few extra minutes comes in handy if unexpected complications arise. Second, attention should be paid both to the form and content of what the patient is saying. One might note that the patient is reticent or effusive, suspicious or gullible, and so forth. These bits and pieces of information should be tucked into the back of one's mind to be used either as comparative background or as topics of specific investigation during the evaluation proper. Third, it is advisable to involve the patient in choosing the time for the first appointment. Asking such questions as, "How urgent do you think the situation is?" or "When were you planning to see me?" allows the patient some control and

subtly emphasizes the mutuality of the therapeutic undertaking. Fourth, if the patient places conditions upon coming in, these should be met neither by undue flexibility nor by dogmatic rigidity. A firm adherence to neutrality, curiosity, and respect for the complexity of mental phenomena is what is required. Fifth, it is considerate to inform the patient right away of any constraints from one's own side. For instance, if one does not have time to take on a new patient, it is wise to let the patient know that on the phone rather than during or after the evaluation. Or, if someone calls for an appointment when one is about to go away for a while, it seems reasonable to inform the patient of the upcoming interruption and perhaps not even begin an evaluation before the break. Finally, one should give clear directions about the location of one's office and not assume that the patient knows his way around.

(2) *Observing the patient's appearance, behavior, and manner of arrival*: Nonverbal behaviors (a sudden avoidance of eye contact, an increase in fidgetiness, etc.) often reveal significant information during the clinical interview. However, there are things to be observed even before the interview has begun. Is the patient appropriately dressed? Are there outstanding mannerisms, scars, or tattoos? Does he look angry, sad, happy? Does he come on time? Does he come accompanied by someone? Does he bring too many things with him? What feelings does he stir up in us right away? All this should be considered data. While it may not always prove worthwhile, it cannot be flatly ignored. Indeed, at times, such observations can lead to major discoveries about the patient.

SUGGESTED READINGS

Akhtar, S. (1992). *Broken Structures: Severe Personality Disorders and Their Treatment*, pp. 275–307. Northvale, NJ: Jason Aronson.

Gabbard, G. (1990). *Psychodynamic Psychiatry in Clinical Practice*, pp. 49–69. Washington, DC: American Psychiatric Press.

Mackinnon, R. A., and Michels, R. (1971). *The Psychiatric Interview in Clinical Practice*. Philadelphia: W. B. Saunders.

48. How does one assess issues of identity in the clinical interview?

The main distinguishing feature between a neurotic and a border-line level of personality is the degree of identity consolidation the individual has achieved. In neurotic character organization, identity is well established and defenses center on repression while in borderline organization, there is identity diffusion and a predominance of splitting. The assessment of identity consolidation is, therefore, of crucial importance in arriving at a characterological diagnosis.

The features of identity diffusion include markedly contradictory character traits, temporal discontinuity in the self-experience, feelings of emptiness, gender dysphoria, subtle body-image disturbances, and inordinate ethnic and moral relativism. *Not all of these features can be elicited and explored to an equal degree through formal questioning.* Some (e.g., feelings of emptiness) are more evident in the patient's complaints, while others (e.g., temporal discontinuity in the self-experience) become clear only through obtaining a longitudinal account of the patient's life. Still other features (e.g., subtle disturbances of gender identity) are discernible, at least in the beginning, mainly through the overall manner of the patient's relating to the interviewer. *Yet it is almost always helpful to ask the patient to describe himself or herself.* Of course, such an inquiry begins only after the patient's presenting symptomatology has been discussed. At this point, the interviewer might say something like this: "Well, now that you have told me about your difficulties and we have talked about them for a while, can you please describe yourself as a person?" In the description offered, one should look for consistency versus contradiction, clarity versus confusion, solidity versus emptiness, well-developed and comfortably experienced masculinity or femininity versus gender confusion, and a sense of inner morality and ethnicity versus the lack of any historical or communal anchor.

However, if the patient is unable to provide a coherent self-description, this should not be automatically construed as showing identity diffusion. It could be due to anxiety, lack of psychological mindedness, cultural factors, poor verbal skills, or low intelligence. These factors should be ruled out before making a conclusion regarding the presence or absence of identity diffusion. Moreover, *a less than forthcoming patient is often helped in this regard by a piecemeal inquiry.* For instance, the interviewer might ask about the patient's religious beliefs, practices, and their continuity with what was handed down to him during childhood; feelings of ethnicity and of belonging to a certain regional or communal group; continuity with friends and associates from earlier periods of life; clarity and stability of vocational goals; sublimations and hobbies; legal record; drug use and drinking, and so on. He may then surmise information about the patient's identity based on the material gathered. *A patient might not be able to describe himself well, yet may turn out to possess a consolidated identity.* Conversely, one might come across in a patient

> peripheral areas of self-experience that are contradictory to a well-integrated, central area of subjective experience, peripheral areas that the patient experiences as ego-alien or ego-dystonic, not fitting into his otherwise integrated picture of himself. These isolated areas may be an important source of intrapsychic conflict or interpersonal difficulties but should not be equated with identity diffusion. [Kernberg 1984, p. 37]

SUGGESTED READINGS

Akhtar, S. (1984). The syndrome of identity diffusion. *American Journal of Psychiatry* 141:1381–1385.

Kernberg, O. F. (1970). A psychoanalytic classification of character pathology. *Journal of the American Psychoanalytic Association* 15:641–685.

——— (1984). *Severe Personality Disorders: Psychotherapeutic Strategies*, pp. 27–51. New Haven, CT: Yale University Press.

49. How does one assess the depth of the patient's object relations?

The actual nature of the patient's object relations becomes evident only through its unfolding in the transference–countertransference axis during psychotherapeutic or psychoanalytic treatment. However, it is possible, indeed necessary and beneficial, to have some sense of the patient's capacities in this regard from the very beginning.

In order to develop an understanding of the patient's internal object relations, the interviewer should review the patient's interpersonal relationships, including those of childhood as well as the current life. In addition, the interviewer must keep an eye on how the patient relates to him during the interview itself. He might ask the patient to describe his or her mother and father in some detail. Current relationships should also be subjected to a similar scrutiny. Asking the patient to describe a spouse, a friend, an employer and so on provides a ready-made access to pertinent intrapsychic information. The existence of the following three features in the patient's descriptions of significant individuals, from childhood and/or current life, suggests primitive object relations and therefore hints at a lower level of character organization.

(1) *An emphasis upon one's own feelings and views about the person one is describing rather than on that person's actual, independent attributes*: For instance, in response to an inquiry such as, "Can you tell me what sort of a person your father is?", the patient with impaired capacity of object relations tends to respond by statements like "Actually I do not like him," or "I simply adore him." In contrast, an individual with deeper object relations tends to respond with, "My father is a serious and somewhat reserved individual who. . . ." Not only does the person with impaired object relations fail to adequately describe his father (or, for that matter, his mother, brother, spouse, etc.) as a

separate and distinct individual, often he or she can not even do so after prompting in that direction from the interviewing clinician. (2) *An extreme and affectively charged verdict rather than a balanced account that permits mixed feelings toward the individual being described*: Individuals with shallow object relations tend to make statements like, "He is a son of a bitch," "She is the world's best," and so on. Those who are capable of experiencing others as whole objects having both good and bad qualities speak differently of them. Their descriptions are along the lines of, "My father is a decent, hard-working man but a bit miserly and socially awkward," or "To tell you the truth, my wife is a rather miserable and chronically irritable person but she is a talented pianist and an unbelievable cook," and so on. A simple yet profound guide in listening to the patient's descriptions of others is to watch for the occurrence of qualifying phrases such as "but," "yet," "however," "at the same time," and so forth. These give voice to the underlying capacity to integrate, at least to a certain extent, contradictory representations of internalized objects.

(3) *An inability to see independent motivations in others*: Compare the statement, "My wife does not keep up her appearance because she knows it bugs me," with "My wife does not keep up her appearance because coming from a very poor family, she just cannot bring herself to spend money on cosmetics." The issue is not that the patient's explanations are correct, but that they show an ability to consider that others might have reasons of their own.

Asking patients to describe significant others in their lives and scanning their reports along these three parameters helps in evaluating the depth of their object relations.

SUGGESTED READINGS

Akhtar, S. (1992). *Broken Structures: Severe Personality Disorders and Their Treatment*, pp. 275–307. Northvale, NJ: Jason Aronson.

Gabbard, G. (1990). *Psychodynamic Psychiatry in Clinical Practice*, pp. 49–69. Washington, DC: American Psychiatric Press.

Kernberg O. F. (1984). *Severe Personality Disorders: Psychotherapeutic Strategies*, pp. 27–51. New Haven, CT: Yale University Press.

50. What is meant by *safeguarding the therapeutic framework*?

An important task during the initial interview, besides collecting information, is to establish, preserve, and protect the therapeutic framework. This is accomplished by maintaining curiosity without being intrusive, showing firmness tempered by flexibility, and insisting on honesty without becoming moralistic. Confronting pathological defenses and appealing to the healthy sector of the patient's personality are also important constituents of such an approach. While the interviewer seeks to stay in this position, a patient's naïveté and/or psychopathology pulls his work ego away from it. No hard-and-fast rules exist for dealing with complex situations that arise as a result. However, there are two useful guidelines: (1) the interview should be conducted with a firm adherence to technical neutrality, and (2) a temporary giving up of neutrality is preferable to risking harm to the patient or oneself, carrying on an interview under bizarre circumstances, and colluding with a pathological agenda. The paradox between the two guidelines is as obvious as it is unavoidable. A few examples of handling tricky situations during the initial evaluation might illustrate this point.

(1) A minor situation occurs when a patient asks for permission to smoke during the session. In such a situation the therapist might respond with something like, "No, you may not smoke a cigarette. If you wish, I will gladly explain the reasons for my stance." If the patient takes one up on this offer, one might say that "smoking is harmful to one's health and by permitting it I would be colluding with your self neglect. Moreover, for the kind of work we have undertaken today, some degree of tension is necessary. Anxiety is the fuel of our work and your smoking, by diminishing it, will render our work pale." (Depending on the degree of the patient's psychological mindedness and the affective tone in the interview, one might also invite the patient to be

curious about the timing of his request.) On the other hand, if such a request is made by a patient who is truly panicked and becoming psychotic in front of one's eyes, one might permit smoking.

(2) A more serious situation occurs when a patient refuses to give identifying information about himself while insisting on talking about his problems. Such a stance is neither acceptable nor unacceptable. The interviewer should explore with the patient the reasons for his desire to remain incognito. If these appear convincing (e.g., the patient is a relocated government witness and is not legally permitted to reveal his name) and resilient (i.e., the patient is able to consider revealing his real name as the work proceeds and trust deepens), the interviewer might proceed even without knowing the patient's real name. On the other hand, if the patient cannot conceptualize ever revealing his real name and seems to be grossly lying, the evaluator needs to put a firm limit on this behavior, including possibly terminating the interview altogether.

(3) Finally, if a patient mentions suicidal ideation, the interviewer should explore it with equanimity. However, if the patient reveals a definite suicidal plan during the evaluative interview, active preventive measures, often at the cost of aborting the interview proper, need to be taken.

These three examples are meant to illustrate that safeguarding the therapeutic framework is as integral a part of the diagnostic interview as collecting descriptive information or generating dynamic hypotheses.

SUGGESTED READINGS

Akhtar, S. *Broken Structures: Severe Personality Disorders and Their Treatment*, pp. 277–307. Northvale, NJ: Jason Aronson.

Kernberg, O. F. (1984). *Severe Personality Disorders: Psychotherapeutic Strategies*, pp. 27–52. New Haven, CT: Yale University Press.

Mackinnon, R. A., and Michels, R. (1971). *The Psychiatric Interview in Clinical Practice*. Philadelphia: W. B. Saunders.

51. What are the ways to assess the patient's psychological mindedness?

Since greater psychological mindedness is associated with the favorable outcome of any insight-oriented treatment, its assessment becomes an important task during the initial evaluation. But what is psychological mindedness? Morton Reiser (1971) sees it as consisting of: (1) sensitivity to symbolic meanings and to resemblances between life events in historical context, (2) empathy for others' affective experiences, and (3) interest in motives that underlie human behavior. Psychological mindedness is more inwardly directed, reflective, and receptive than curiosity, which is outwardly directed, driving, and compelling. David Werman (1979), in contrast, noted that psychological mindedness is evident not only in one's capacity for self-observation but also in one's view of the external world. The inability to accept chance occurrences and the intolerance of ambiguity in the external world are often the outward manifestations of poor psychological mindedness.

The most detailed guidelines for assessing psychological mindedness in the diagnostic interview were provided by Nina Coltart (1988). She outlined nine points under two headings: the history, and developments in the interview. Under the first heading, Coltart suggests that one should look for

1. The capacity to give a history which deepens, acquires more coherence, and becomes textually more substantial as it goes on. . . . 2. The capacity to give such a history without much prompting, and a history which gives the listener an increasing awareness that the patient feels currently related in himself, to his own story. . . . 3. The capacity to bring up memories with appropriate affects. [p. 819]

Under the second heading, Coltart includes the following:

4. Some awareness in the patient that he has an unconscious mental life. . . . 5. Some capacity to step back, if only momentarily, from self-experience, and to observe it reflectively. . . . 6. A capacity, or more strongly a wish, to accept and handle increased responsibility for the self. . . . 7. Imagination. . . . 8. Some capacity for achievement, and some realistic self-esteem. . . . 9. Overall impression . . . something deeply recognizable, but ultimately not fully definable, about the assessor's experience of a thorough, intense, working consultation with a psychologically minded person. [pp. 819–820]

To summarize, it seems that psychological mindedness is best assessed by observing the following items: (1) *capacity for reflective self-observation* as evidenced by the patient's giving a coherent and affectively resonant history and by his or her ability to be aware (or become aware during the interview) of internal conflicts; (2) *interest in one's mental life* as evidenced by a history of having kept journals, and by spontaneously mentioning dreams and fantasies in the initial interview; (3) *belief in psychic causality* as evidenced by the patient's offering a genetic explanation of his or her own or another's behavior and by a capacity to entertain a mental basis for certain accidents, onset of a physical illness, and so on; (4) *ability to accept ambiguity and chance occurrences* in external reality without feeling compelled to explain everything; and (5) *readiness to see symbolic meanings* and enter into a metaphorical dialogue as evidenced by a positive, even welcoming, response to a trial interpretation.

SUGGESTED READINGS

Coltart, N. E. (1988). The assessment of psychological-mindedness in the diagnostic interview. *British Journal of Psychiatry* 153:819–820.

Reiser, M. F. (1971). Psychological issues in training for research in psychiatry. *Journal of Psychiatric Review* 8:531–537.

Werman, D. S. (1979). Chance, ambiguity, and psychological mindedness. *Psychoanalytic Quarterly* 48:107–115.

52. How should the initial evaluation be concluded?

The initial evaluation enters its terminal phase once the core information has been gathered, a working hypothesis about the nature of the patient's suffering has been developed, and the patient's psychological mindedness has been assessed. *At this point, the interviewer should inform the patient that the evaluation is over and share his conclusions with the patient in jargon-free language.* He might include in his comments hints of how he arrived at his conclusions. Quoting something the patient had said, recounting a particular emotional outburst, reminding the patient of a slip of the tongue, and so on, enhance the patient's sense of participation and mutuality even at this phase. This, in turn, facilitates the patient's receptivity to the information being given.

It might also be useful, besides being true, to preface one's comments with the caveat that conclusions arrived at in one to three sessions are necessarily a bit tentative. The interviewer might also bring up the need for further investigations of a social (i.e., family interview), psychometric, or laboratory kind, if he thinks that these might help to clarify the situation. While the use of colloquial language is preferable in discussing this, there is no reason to be wishy-washy or apologetic if a patient asks for a specific psychiatric diagnosis. Exploring the patient's reasons for asking might reveal further significant information. However, such exploration should not be used as a delay tactic, and a patient who wants to know his diagnosis should be told. Much is made of a patient's misunderstanding of diagnostic terminology or being narcissistically injured by it. What is overlooked is that the interviewer's cryptic attitude, fudging, or avoidance can also have alienating and adverse effects on the patient.

Following the discussion of the nature of the patient's problems, the focus should shift to treatment. The interviewer should now inform the patient of the ideal treatment for the malady, explaining, especially if asked, the reasons for this recommendation. The patient should also be informed of alternate approaches to treating the condition. Questions raised by the patient should be answered factually, and the interviewer should not derail or mystify the patient by interpreting the reasons behind such questions. For instance, if a patient asks about the difference between psychoanalysis and psychotherapy, one might explain the difference in terms of frequency of visits, the use of the couch, and the nature of the patient's and therapist's expected roles.

Once the treatment strategy has been discussed, the interviewer should explore with the patient the feasibility of carrying it out. This would necessitate a review of the patient's schedule, financial resources, geographical stability, and ease of arriving at the therapist's office, and so on. Equipped with this information, the interviewer can fine-tune his recommendations. At this point, based on the nature of the treatment modality selected and/or the patient's external reality, one may elect to treat the patient oneself or may suggest a referral elsewhere if necessary. In the former instance, and especially if there is no crisis at hand, it is good to give the patient some additional time to mull over the consultation and the agreed-upon treatment plan. After this interval, a meeting should be held to discuss practical arrangements (schedule, fees, method of emergency communication, etc.), as well as to explain what is expected of the patient in order for the therapeutic work to be optimally helpful. With this accomplished, treatment can begin.

SUGGESTED READINGS

Akhtar, S. (1992). *Broken Structures: Severe Personality Disorders and Their Treatment*, pp. 277–307. Northvale, NJ: Jason Aronson.

Kernberg, O. F. (1984). *Severe Personality Disorders: Psychotherapeutic Strategies*, pp. 27–51. New Haven, CT: Yale University Press.

Yeomans, F. E., Selzer, M. A., and Clarkin, J. F. (1992). *Treating the Borderline Patient*. New York: Basic Books.

53. What is a *structural interview*?

The term *structural interview* was introduced into the psychoanalytic and psychiatric literature by Otto Kernberg in 1981. Essentially it refers to a *specific method of initial evaluation of patients that differs from the traditional history taking in important ways.* These differences emanate from the purpose of the interview. The structural interview is not meant only to establish a descriptive diagnosis. It is aimed at sharpening a psychostructural differential diagnosis, thus highlighting therapeutic and prognostic implications. "It tells us about the patient's motivation, his capacity for introspection and for collaboration in psychotherapeutic treatment, and his potential for acting out and for psychotic decompensation" (Kernberg 1984, p. 27).

A clinician conducting a structural interview begins by asking the patient to present a brief summary of his reasons for seeking help and his expectations of treatment. As the patient responds, the interviewer not only gathers facts but also notes the degree of cohesion in the material offered. If the patient can describe the situation in a realistic way, the interviewer can discard potentially psychotic illness as a diagnosis. When there is vagueness or excessive concreteness, the interviewer seeks a clarification of the discrepancy between his questions and the patient's responses. If the patient acknowledges difficulty in following the interviewer's questions, the interviewer not only repeats them in different wordings but also explores the nature of the patient's difficulty. Then *the interviewer moves on to explore the potential existence of related symptoms. This is followed by an investigation of character traits, especially the presence or absence of identity diffusion.* If the patient displays a well-synthesized, deep, and ambivalent view of himself, the interview can usually rule out a borderline personality organization. If, on the other hand, the patient has difficulty in describing himself, the interview explores the potential cultural and/or psychological aspects of this difficulty. The interviewer might then attempt a more piecemeal exploration of the patient's identity and, failing in that, conclude the existence of borderline personality organization.

The next question deals with significant others in the patient's life. Patients with borderline personality organization, when faced with such a question, display an incapacity to integrate the representations of others in depth; they have trouble in presenting affectively rich, three-dimensional descriptions of others. When contradictions appear in the patient's descriptions of others, the interviewer tactfully brings them up and assesses the patient's capacity to reflect on the interviewer's observations. While this part of the interview is proceeding, the interviewer also silently observes the effects of his confrontations and clarifications upon the evolving relationship between him and the patient in the here and now of the clinical situation. With neurotic patients, the increase in anxiety and mobilization of the patient's usual defenses is mostly unobtrusive. In borderline patients, however, primitive defenses begin to alter and distort the interview itself.

In essence, *the structural interview simultaneously involves exploring the patient's inner world, observing the patient's interaction with the interviewer, and utilizing the interviewer's own affective responses for the purpose of clarification and trial interpretations.* To carry it out successfully requires knowledge and experience as well as a reasonable amount of time. However, its rewards are ample and its technique can be learned. An important first step is a careful study of the following references.

SUGGESTED READINGS

Kernberg, O. F. (1981). Structural interviewing. *Psychiatric Clinics of North America* 4:169–195.

―――― (1984). *Severe Personality Disorders: Psychotherapeutic Strategies*, pp. 27–51. New Haven, CT: Yale University Press.

Kernberg, O. F., Goldstein, E., Carr, A., et al. (1981). Diagnosing borderline personality organization. *Journal of Nervous and Mental Disease* 169:225–231.

54. What are the indications for hospitalization?

An important early decision pertains to treating the patient as an outpatient or as an inpatient. A pivotal consideration here is that of *associated psychosis*. Individuals with severe personality disorders often seek help during transient psychotic regressions which are either drug-related or stress-induced. The treatment of such psychotic symptomatology takes precedence over that of the underlying personality disorder (Kernberg, 1984) and raises the question of hospitalization. The presence of psychosis in the setting of limited social supports generally indicates the need for hospitalization. If the psychotic symptoms are mild, ample social networks exist, and the patient is willing to comply with the recommended psychotropic regime, then hospitalization may be avoided.

An assessment of *suicidal risk* is also necessary in considering hospitalization. If the patient is suicidal, then the decision is clearly in favor of hospitalization (voluntary or involuntary). If the patient is not suicidal, then the treatment can be conducted on an outpatient basis. However, a clinical challenge is posed by situations in which the extent of suicidal risk is unclear. Here, it is helpful to remember that there are five Ds (*drinking, drug abuse*, severe *depression*, physical *disease* or deformity, and *disorganized* social life leading to anomie and isolation) that suggest a problematic outcome (Akhtar 1992). When a dubiously suicidal patient displays even two or three of these symptoms, it is preferable to err on the side of caution and choose hospitalization. At the same time, the extent to which the patient has been honest during the evaluation should be considered. That the patient is dishonest is often revealed by (1) history of withholding information from previous therapists, (2) record of legal offenses, (3) evidence of breaking moral commitments (e.g., an honor code violation on campus or an extramarital affair), (4) gross discrepancies in the historical account provided by the patient and others, and (5) the patient's resistance to acknowledging anything about himself that will put him in a socially negative light. If any of these indicators of dishonesty exist, then the patient's information about his suicidal intent cannot be relied on (Kernberg 1984). Under such circumstances, it is preferable to hospitalize him for further evaluation. If the patient refuses voluntary admission, the therapist must initiate involuntary commitment. If this is not granted due to the way in which the pertinent laws are interpreted in a given community, as least the therapist will have tried in good faith to implement what seemed the best treatment option. Such caution and integrity would not only protect the therapist legally, they would minimize his anxiety in assessing alternative ways of managing the situation.

Finally, as Kernberg (1984) emphasizes, distinction should be made between the objectives for short-term and long-term hospitalization. Short-term hospitalization is indicated for averting suicide risk, controlling psychotic symptoms, doing a comprehensive diagnostic workup, mobilizing family supports, and planning future outpatient treatment. Long-term hospitalization, in contrast, is aimed at

> the modification of personality features of these patients that militate against their capacity to engage in and maintain outpatient psychotherapy. The key personality features to be modified in long-term hospital treatment include the patient's attitudes toward his illness and the treatment, that is, lack of introspection or insight, poor motivation for treatment, and significant secondary gain of illness. [Kernberg 1984, p. 173]

SUGGESTED READINGS

Akhtar, S. (1992). *Broken Structures: Severe Personality Disorders and Their Treatment*, pp. 277–307. Northvale, NJ: Jason Aronson.

Kernberg, O. F. (1977). *Borderline Conditions and Pathological Narcissism*, pp. 185–211. New York: Jason Aronson.

_____ (1984). *Severe Personality Disorders: Psychotherapeutic Strategies*, pp. 27–51. New Haven, CT: Yale University Press.

55. What is the role of medication in the treatment of severe personality disorders?

The basic problems of individuals with severe personality disorders are not affected by medication. However, certain of their features do force one to consider psychopharmacologic interventions. First, the genetic links that some of these disorders have with schizophrenia and/or bipolar affective disorder make it tempting to view them as potentially drug-responsive. Second, most such patients seek help during a major crisis and with intense dysphoria; the intensity of their behavior disturbance often warrants the quick alteration offered by various psychotropic medications. Finally, a diagnostic workup often yields results that indicate pharmacologic intervention. These three factors may not only suggest a need for medication but may affect the choice of psychotropic agents used. In any case, one thing is clear: while putting personality disorder patients on medication may reflect the therapist's inexperience and countertransference, this is not always the case. For patients on the severe end of this spectrum, careful, brief, and target symptom-oriented drug intervention might indeed be quite useful. Such interventions include: (1) low-dose antipsychotic agents for transitory psychotic episodes, paranoia, depersonalization, uncontrollable impulsivity, and cognitive disorganization; (2) lithium for affective lability, hypomanic excitement, "hysteroid dysphoria," and refractory depression; (3) tricyclic antidepressants for depression, panic, and compulsive symptoms; and (4) monoamine oxidase inhibitors for agoraphobia, atypical depression, and panic attacks. Other medications, including benzodiazipines, newer antidepressants, beta blockers, carbamezepine, and anticonvulsants, have also been used with personality disordered patients with mixed results.

A careful literature review and consultation with a pharmacologically up-to-date colleague should precede one's use of medications. In any case, there are many caveats about the drug treatment of personality disorders.

> First, drug treatment should not be presented to patients as a panacea — it is better to profess a cautious uncertainty about possible benefit, even if this attitude mitigates placebo effect. Second, careful consideration should be given to risks versus benefits before instituting medication for patients with ongoing substance abuse, suicidal ideation, or inability to comply with required diet, blood levels, dosing schedule, or follow-up visits. Third, a consistent focus on unrealistic expectations is crucial to maximize both compliance and evaluation of efficacy. Fourth, concurrent treatments should remain firmly in place because drug therapy alone is rarely globally effective. Fifth, drugs should be introduced into treatment as a single variable: they should be used for preplanned periods with a clear beginning and end-point related to agreed-on target symptoms. Sixth, serial substitution of alternative drugs is preferable to concurrent use of alternative drugs. Seventh, drugs and dosages that may cause tardive dyskinesia, paradoxical dyscontrol, or lowering of seizure threshold should, if possible, be reserved as final treatment options. Eighth, informed consent for drug trials should be obtained continually over the course of treatment. Ninth, worsening symptoms should alert the clinician to the possible presence of some other disorder, a negative therapeutic reaction, a drug interaction with illicit agents, paradoxical aggravation of target symptoms, or the presence of an undiagnosed mental illness. [Gorton and Akhtar 1990, p. 47]

SUGGESTED READINGS

Gorton, G., and Akhtar, S. (1990). The literature on personality disorders, 1985–88: trends, issues, and controversies. *Hospital and Community Psychiatry* 41:39–51.

Liebowitz, M. R., Stone, M., and Turkat, I. (1986). Treatment of personality disorders. In *Psychiatry Update: American Psychiatric Association Annual Review*, vol. 5, ed. A. Frances and R. Hales, pp. 356–393. Washington, DC: American Psychiatric Press.

Stone, M. H. (1983). Borderline personality disorder. In *New Psychiatric Syndromes: DSM-III and Beyond*, ed. S. Akhtar, pp. 19–48. New York: Jason Aronson.

56. Is psychoanalysis indicated for individuals with severe character pathology?

From a systematic review of sixteen clinical and eight quantitative-predictive studies of analyzability, Henry Bachrach and Louis Leaff (1978) concluded that *individuals most suitable for psychoanalysis* have good ego strength, intact reality testing, capacity for sublimation. They are able to cope flexibly, communicate verbally, and regress in the service of the ego with sufficiently intact thinking to negotiate the tasks of psychoanalysis. Their symptoms are mild and their diagnoses fall within a neurotic spectrum.

> Such persons are able to form a transference neurosis and therapeutic alliance, are relatively free of narcissistic pathology, have good object relations with friends, parents, and spouses, and have been able to tolerate early separations and deprivations without impairment of object constancy; they are therefore able to experience genuine triangular conflict. They are motivated for self-understanding, change, and to relieve personal suffering. They are persons with good tolerance for anxiety, depression, frustration, and suffering and are able to experience surges of feeling without loss of impulse control or disruption of secondary-process mooring of thought. Their character attitudes and traits are well-suited to the psychoanalytic, i.e., psychological mindedness. Superego is integrated and tolerant. They are mainly in their late twenties or early thirties and have not experienced past psychotherapeutic failure or difficulties. Of all these qualities, those relating to ego strength and object relations are most important. [pp. 885–886]

Bachrach and Leaff's conclusions have largely been upheld by subsequent studies that reveal that factors indicating analyzability include ego strength, deep object relations, psychological mindedness, achievement of object constancy, realistic expectations, and the capacity for developing both transference and therapeutic alliance. In contrast, "persons not likely to benefit come to analysis seeking magical fulfillments consistent with their infantile attitudes, character traits, and impoverished, need-satisfying relations with people" (Bachrach and Leaff 1978, p. 885).

Two recent developments, however, make the picture somewhat more optimistic. First, there is an increasing awareness that analyzability may depend not only on intrinsic factors in the patient but also on the match between the patient and the analyst. A patient deemed unanalyzable by one analyst may turn out to be analyzable by another. Second, the increasing assimilation into psychoanalytic theory of child observation data and of conceptual models other than traditional structural theory (e.g., object relations theory, self psychology, the Kleinian approach) has led to a more refined and flexible psychoanalytic technique that might be applicable to more severe psychopathology. Kernberg has "recently become more optimistic" (1984, p. 165) in this regard. He feels that narcissistic personalities not functioning on an overt borderline level, and infantile personalities with hysterical features, even when functioning on a borderline level, may be analyzable. The presence of talents, honesty, perseverance, and a genuine desire to change oneself, enhances analyzability in the setting of severe character pathology. However, even with this optimistic note, the fact remains that psychoanalysis is indicated for only a small proportion of those with severe personality disorders.

SUGGESTED READINGS

Bachrach, H., and Leaff, L. (1978). "Analyzability": a systematic review of the clinical and quantitative literature. *Journal of the American Psychoanalytic Association* 26:881–920.

Erle, J., and Goldberg, D. A. (1984). Observations on the assessment of analyzability by experienced analysts. *Journal of the American Psychoanalytic Association* 32:715–737.

Kernberg, O. (1984). *Severe Personality Disorders: Psychotherapeutic Strategies*, pp. 165–176. New Haven, CT: Yale University Press.

57. What are the indications for psychoanalytic psychotherapy?

Psychoanalytic psychotherapy is the treatment of choice for most patients with severe personality disorders. However, they must meet certain basic criteria including (1) at least normal intelligence, (2) psychological mindedness, especially as evidenced in their thoughtful and self-reflective responses to trial interpretations during the initial evaluation, (3) honesty, (4) absence of significant drug abuse and drinking, (5) a track record of task-related perseverance, (6) willingness and ability to attend two to three sessions per week for a reasonably long length of time, possibly two to three years, and (7) reasonably stable external circumstances so that minimal structuring of the treatment is necessary. In addition, the therapist should have ready access to an inpatient setting and to support personnel who, if needed, can make environmental interventions on his behalf and thus safeguard his neutrality.

A similar, though somewhat more extensive, list is provided by Gabbard (1990), who suggests that the presence of the following eleven features indicates an expressive, exploratory emphasis in psychotherapy:

(1) strong motivation to understand, (2) significant suffering, (3) ability to regress in the service of the ego, (4) tolerance for frustration, (5) capacity for insight (psychological mindedness), (6) intact reality testing, (7) meaningful object relations, (8) good impulse control, (9) ability to sustain work, (10) capacity to think in terms of analogy and metaphor, and (11) reflective responses to trial interpretations. [p. 88]

Gabbard emphasizes that in practice most patients present some, not all, of these indications.

Specific phenomenological constellations within the severe personality disorder spectrum also play a role here. While well-functioning narcissistic personalities and patients manifesting mixed infantile (histrionic) and hysterical features are suitable for psychoanalysis proper, other forms of severe character pathology are better served by psychoanalytic psychotherapy. Thus, those with narcissistic personality with overt borderline features, mixed narcissistic and paranoid features, schizoid personality, and borderline personality are more suitable candidates for psychoanalytic psychotherapy than for psychoanalysis proper. In addition, patients who display

> severe chronic self-destructiveness (such as self-mutilating tendencies, suicidal tendencies as a "way of life," and anorexia nervosa are suitable for this type of psychotherapy, if sufficient external structure can be provided to prevent or control acting out that may otherwise threaten the continuation of the treatment or the patient's life. [Kernberg 1984, p. 167]

Severely antisocial personalities, hypomanic personalities, and "as-if" personalities with pronounced tendencies toward pathological lying are, in contrast, not viable candidates for psychoanalytic psychotherapy. It seems that the general requirements of motivation, honesty, verbal facility, intelligence, and absence of significant substance abuse cut across these diagnostic categories when it comes to selecting a therapeutic strategy. However, the true test of the patient's suitability is in his participation in the treatment process itself. Sometimes, a carefully selected individual turns out to be unsuitable for psychoanalytic psychotherapy. At other times, what appeared a dubious candidate surprises us positively. The guidelines outlined here, therefore, need to be tempered by the therapist's disciplined courage, his overall clinical experience, and the "fit" between himself and the patient.

SUGGESTED READINGS

Akhtar, S. (1992). *Broken Structures: Severe Personality Disorders and Their Treatment*, pp. 275–307. Northvale, NJ: Jason Aronson.

Gabbard, G. (1990). *Psychodynamic Psychiatry in Clinical Practice*, pp. 71–99. Washington, DC: American Psychiatric Press.

Kernberg, O. F. (1984). *Severe Personality Disorders: Psychotherapeutic Strategies*, pp. 167–168. New Haven, CT: Yale University Press.

58. Are there contraindications to initiating intensive psychotherapy?

Yes. These contraindications are usually relative and not absolute and involve both external and internal factors.

(1) *External factors*: Certain realistic conditions must be met before one agrees to treat a patient in intensive psychotherapy. Some certainty of sustained financial resources, for instance, is necessary. Another requirement is the patient's willingness and ability to regularly attend the required number of sessions per week. The patient's residing within a reasonable distance of the therapist's office is therefore helpful. In the absence of these basic requirements of money, attendance, and ease of travel, it is preferable not to accept the patient for treatment. A patient who lives a long distance from the therapist's office might make earnest promises to maintain regular attendance for the sessions. Such resolve, well-meaning though it might be in the beginning, is soon eroded by bad weather, traffic difficulties, and, more important, the emergence of negative transference and resistance during treatment. Rather than accepting such a patient for treatment, the therapist should encourage him or her to seek help at a more geographically reasonable locale. Even in those rare situations in which such help is truly not available nearby, the patient should be offered psychotherapeutic help on an emergency basis only, instead of acceptance in an ongoing regular treatment conducted far away in a less than optimal fashion. On the other hand, one must be willing to reconsider the treatment strategy should there be a change in the patient's residential status.

Yet another situation that should preclude the patient's acceptance for intensive treatment occurs when there is an impending move in the patient's near future. It may be worthwhile to explore with the patient the conflict underlying this seeking of help while planning to leave town. This may identify for the patient (and the therapist) hitherto unrecognized anxieties regarding intimacy and distance (Akhtar 1992). While such information might become a useful nidus for future treatment, the temptation to start a brief but "deep" treatment while the patient is leaving town in a few weeks or months must be resisted.

(2) *Internal factors*: Besides the above-mentioned difficulties in external reality, there are internal factors that should give the therapist pause before accepting a patient for intensive psychotherapeutic intervention. Pronounced antisocial tendencies are almost always a contraindication to in-depth treatment (Kernberg 1984). A markedly deficient capacity for verbal communication, regardless of its etiology, also precludes such intervention. Low intelligence levels do the same. Prominent financial and legal secondary gains from the illness are usually indicators of problematic developments during the course of psychotherapy and should therefore be regarded as potential contraindications to such treatment. Excessive drinking, significant drug abuse, stubborn refusal to attend sessions as recommended, and relentless sadomasochistic acting out also constitute contraindications. However, with a firm initial contract (Selzer et al. 1987) and with concurrent institution of adjunctive treatment measures (e.g., medications, Alcoholics Anonymous, or hospitalization), it may be possible to engage some of these patients in a meaningful, long-term treatment.

SUGGESTED READINGS

Akhtar, S. (1992). Tethers, orbits, and invisible fences: clinical, developmental, sociocultural, and technical aspects of optimal distance. In *When the Body Speaks: Psychological Meanings in Kinetic Clues*, ed. S. Kramer and S. Akhtar, pp. 21–57. Northvale, NJ: Jason Aronson.

Kernberg, O. F. (1984). *Severe Personality Disorders: Psychotherapeutic Strategies*, pp. 165–176. New Haven, CT: Yale University Press.

Selzer, M. A., Koenigsberg, H. W., and Kernberg, O. F. (1987). The initial contract in the treatment of borderline patients. *American Journal of Psychiatry* 144:927–930.

59. When is supportive psychotherapy indicated?

This is a controversial matter. Kernberg (1984) asserts that "supportive psychotherapy is rarely if ever the treatment modality of choice" (p. 168) for individuals with severe personality disorders. He goes on to add that "as a general rule the indication for supportive psychotherapy for these patients derives from the contraindication for expressive psychotherapy" (p. 168). Kernberg holds that such intervention is only indicated if the patient lacks motivation, psychological mindedness, or ability to participate in the two to three sessions per week required for psychoanalytic psychotherapy. However, these difficulties should not be taken on face value and should be dynamically explored before being accepted as such. More important, intense disorganization of the patient's external life and the existence of severe social isolation tend to indicate supportive psychotherapy.

In contrast, certain other investigators (Adler 1982, Luborsky 1984) believe that supportive psychotherapy might be the treatment of choice for some patients with severe personality disorders. Included in this category are individuals who show (1) a great propensity for acting out, (2) cognitive disorganization with a potentially organic substrate, (3) lack of psychological mindedness, (4) profoundly impaired object relations and a questionable ability to form a therapeutic alliance, (5) severe social isolation, and (6) the existence in their lives of a major, current crisis situation. Patients who meet these criteria are rarely suitable for exploratory or insight-oriented psychotherapy. They require too many environmental interventions, lack observing egos, develop psychotic transferences, and act out in dangerous ways if treated in an insight-oriented manner.

Two other things need to be kept in mind. First, the severity of some of these features might rule out the possibility of undertaking even supportive psychotherapy. Kernberg (1984) notes that:

chronic lying (even without an antisocial personality structure), a history of negative therapeutic reactions with violent aggressive behavior and destructive or self-destructive acts, and relentless masochistic acting out all may raise doubts whether any kind of psychotherapy could be initiated on an outpatient basis. A period of brief or extended hospitalization may clarify these issues and significantly broaden the potential range for all psycho-therapeutic interventions. [p. 169]

Second, while the supportive and psychoanalytic psychotherapies are regarded here as categorically distinct, the fact is that admixtures do exist. To be sure, in their pure forms they do differ considerably. Psychoanalytic psychotherapy analyzes transferences, supportive psychotherapy deflects them. Psychoanalytic psychotherapy avoids persuasion and reassurance, supportive psychotherapy relies on them. Psychoanalytic psychotherapy uses interpretation in addition to confrontation and clarification, the interventions characteristic of supportive psychotherapy. At the same time, it must be emphasized that the therapist's capacity to oscillate freely between ego-supportive and insight-oriented strategies is one of the most important ingredients of therapeutic work with severely ill patients. Moments of crisis, regression, and affective storm are better responded to by containing and holding interventions. These affirm and validate the psychic actuality of the patient's experience, and the resultant ego strengthening, in turn, prepares ground for interpretative exploration. A categorical separation of supportive and psychoanalytic psychotherapies, while useful, should not obliterate the therapist's inner freedom in tailoring his interventions to a specific patient's specific needs at specific times during treatment.

SUGGESTED READINGS

Adler, G. (1982). Supportive psychotherapy revisited. *Hillside Journal of Clinical Psychiatry* 4:3–13.

Kernberg, O. F. (1984). *Severe Personality Disorders: Psychotherapeutic Strategies*, pp. 167–168. New Haven, CT: Yale University Press.

Luborsky, L. (1984). *Principles of Psychoanalytic Psychotherapy: A Manual for Supportive-Expressive Treatment*. New York: Basic Books.

60. Are family and group interventions ever useful in the treatment of borderline individuals?

As adjunct measures to individual psychotherapy, both family and group interventions can be of considerable benefit in the treatment of borderline individuals. *Work with family* can be useful in both inpatient and outpatient settings. For instance, during the hospitalization of a borderline patient, meeting with family members provides the clinician a direct opportunity to observe pathogenic family interactions that perpetuate and unwittingly reinforce the patient's problematic behaviors. It might also reveal the need of treatment for other family members either individually or, in the case of the parents, as a couple. Supportive and structure-building family interventions might also be required around discharge planning. Involving the family is also a necessary step in managing chronically suicidal patients on an outpatient basis. A firm clarification of the realistic limits of outpatient psychotherapy and of the potentially risky nature of such patients' psychopathology, in the presence of the family members, is a good way to protect the treatment from unwanted intrusions, while minimizing the therapist's paranoid fears regarding legal actions by third parties. Finally, in families where interpersonal enmeshment is the pervasive pattern and where any improvement on the patient's part appears to seriously threaten the family homeostasis, more formal family therapy is indicated. What must be kept in mind here is that even a pathological homeostasis has adaptive aspects, and the family therapist's efforts, however valiant and well-meaning, to induce a psychic separation between the patient and his family can be grave threats to the system's integrity. Therapeutic work should therefore focus on empathizing with the family's needs and only later on encouraging developmental initiatives of the patient.

Group therapy might also be a beneficial adjunct in the treatment of borderline individuals. It helps reduce the intensity of transference feelings in the context of individual psychotherapy.

Such "dilution" may, at times, be quite useful. It might permit the patient to retain the capacity for self-observation instead of getting affectively drowned in his transference distortions. Moreover, borderline patients appear more accepting of confrontation of their provocative and mistrustful attitudes from their peers in group psychotherapy than from their individual therapist. Of course, if the individual therapist receives detailed feedback from the group therapist, so that the possibility of splitting between the two therapies is minimized, group therapy may actually enrich the individual psychotherapeutic experience. However, a few caveats should be kept in mind. First, the patient should not be in individual therapy with his group therapist. Not only might the juggling of roles, context-based behaviors, and transferences tax the patient's ego adversely, but having such special access to the group therapist might undermine his participation in the group work. Second, it is advisable to place a borderline patient in a group composed of less sick individuals. Third, the group's tendency to scapegoat a borderline patient should be monitored and the patient provided enough ego support during such times. Finally, having intense attachments to their individual therapists, borderline patients might not reveal deeper material in group settings. This tendency should be handled with tact and regard for optimal distance.

SUGGESTED READINGS

Brown, S. L. (1987). Family therapy and the borderline patient. In *The Borderline Patient: Emerging Concepts in Diagnosis, Psychodynamics, and Treatment*, vol. 2, ed. J. S. Grotstein, M. F. Solomon, and J. A. Langs, pp. 206–209. Hillsdale, NJ: Analytic Press.

Gabbard, G. (1990). *Psychodynamic Psychiatry in Clinical Practice*, pp. 49–69. Washington, DC: American Psychiatric Press.

Kernberg, O. F. (1984). *Severe Personality Disorders: Psychotherapeutic Strategies*, pp. 27–51. New Haven, CT: Yale University Press.

Part V

PSYCHOTHERAPY
AND
PSYCHOANALYSIS

61. What are the various approaches to psychoanalytic psychotherapy of severe personality disorders?

As psychoanalysts gradually and painfully discovered the limitations of the traditional analytic method in treating severe character pathology, they undertook a serious reconsideration not only of the psychoanalytic theory of development and psychopathology but also of the potential modifications of their technique. Two paths emerged as a consequence of such reconsideration. Essentially, these two approaches can be seen as representing the "classic" and the "romantic" visions of man, his destiny, and the nature of his anguish (Strenger 1989).

The first path embodies a synthesis of certain Kleinian notions with contemporary ego psychology and is exemplified by the views of Kernberg (and those who have extended his work: e.g., Selzer, Koenigsberg, Yeomans). The technical approach advocated by these theorists (1) regards drive-based wishes as basic motivation, (2) holds conflict as the psychopathological paradigm, (3) views transference as a reactivation of infantile wishes (and defenses against them), (4) prompts a skeptical listening attitude, (5) yields interventions that address resistance and facilitate psychic unmasking, (6) regards deep regression during treatment undesirable because it contaminates reason, (7) sees acting out as unproductive spilling over into life of material that should be restricted to the verbal transactions of therapy, (8) minimizes the therapist's role as a new object, and (9) considers the goal of treatment to be increased rationality and realism.

The second path is represented by the psychoanalysts of the British Middle Group: e.g., Winnicott and Balint, and their exponents, Guntrip, Khan, Casement, Bollas, Wright, and others in England, and Kohut, Adler, Lewin, and Schulz in this country. The technical approach derived from their views (1) regards unmet developmental needs as the motivational substrate, (2) holds deficit as the main psychopathological substrate, (3) views transference as a healthy search for a new object to facilitate the resumption of arrested development, (4) mobilizes a seemingly naïve credulous listening attitude, (5) yields interventions that, through empathy and reconstruction, emphasize the plausibility of the patient's experience, (6) sees deep regression during treatment as offering the possibility of a psychic rebirth, (7) views acting out as a manifestation of the patient's hope for environmental reparation and, through it, psychostructural change), (8) regards the personal warmth and authenticity of the therapist as the crucial ingredient of treatment, and (9) considers the goal of the treatment to be enhanced authenticity and vitality.

I believe that integrating the two divergent approaches yields the most meaningful therapeutic approach. Attempts at such integration are evident in the writings of Modell and Volkan. Modell, while betraying a romantic bent, recognizes the importance of oedipal transferences, a proposition of the classical type. Volkan, though aligned with Kernberg's classic style, acknowledges the redemptive power of deep regression, a proposition of the romantic type. Other hybrid approaches (Killingmo 1989, Strenger 1989) also exist and most clinicians perhaps intuitively strike their own balance between the two positions. I have discussed their integration at length elsewhere (Akhtar 1992), proposing that all clinical material should be seen from both perspectives, and that the choice of which of the two perspectives from which to address the patient should depend on the therapist's intuitive evaluation of the patient's capacity, at that time, to hear and utilize the information imparted.

SUGGESTED READINGS

Akhtar, S. (1992). *Broken Structures: Severe Personality Disorders and Their Treatment*, pp 316–324. Northvale, NJ: Jason Aronson.

Killingmo, B. (1989). Conflict and deficit: implications for technique. *International Journal of Psycho-Analysis* 70:65–79.

Strenger, C. (1989). The classic and romantic visions in psychoanalysis. *International Journal of Psycho-Analysis* 70:595–610.

62. Does the therapist require special skills and personality attributes?

The therapist must be capable of patience, empathy, warmth, and kindness, although, of course, he cannot help individuals with severe personality disorders simply by having these personality attributes. The significance of these qualities is in their complex connections with the therapist's technical skills. Many factors are involved here.

(1) First is the matter of knowledge and experience. While a mastery of basic psychoanalytic theory, developmental concepts, and theory of technique is not essential, a more than elementary knowledge and continued study of these elements is definitely required.

(2) Treating severely ill patients is frequently disheartening. Improvement is slow to occur. For long periods of time, the function of maintaining optimism rests solely with the therapist, who must have "great patience for absence of change" (Kernberg 1984, p. 252), as well as a firmly held conviction that "loss, severe illness, and failure can be tolerated and worked through" (p. 249). Seasoned clinicians draw such conviction from their knowledge and prior experience. The novice, however, must survive on borrowed faith that is, a conviction drawn from the beneficial experience of his own analysis, the useful counsel of his clinical supervisors, and his respectful reading of the prominent works in the field. All three sources function as antidotes to pessimism until grounds for authentic trust in one's work develop.

(3) The therapist must have overcome his narcissistic tendencies. Overcoming his own narcissism prevents him from having unrealistically high expectations from treatment. It also permits him to seek supervision, either on a regular basis or at least during times of doubts and difficulty.

(4) The therapist must be capable of a genuine and specific

emotional response to the patient as well as experiencing a wide range of emotions in general. Such inner freedom not only lends authenticity to his work, it also enhances his capacity to use his countertransference reactions productively.

(5) The therapist must have achieved object constancy. He must be able to integrate, within himself, the patient's contradictory portrayals of him (and the intense emotions that frequently accompany them). When hated, he must be capable of remembering the patient's love for him. When adored, he must not forget the patient's hate of him. Such integration, on his part, will not only reflect in his interpretations but will also help contain and mend the patient's split object relations. An important aspect of this issue is the need for the therapist to be comfortable with aggression, both from within himself and from outside. The therapist's capacity to face his occasional feelings of hostility, even malice, diminishes the chance of his unwittingly putting them into action.

(6) *Finally*, the therapist must firmly adhere to the "principle of multiple function" (Waelder 1936). This helps him accommodate various perspectives on the patient's psychopathology: oedipal versus preoedipal, defensive versus instinctual, conflict versus deficit, hereditary versus environmental, and so forth. The resulting intellectual flexibility prevents the therapist from succumbing to simplistic, either-or, and unifactorial explanations of the psychopathology at hand.

SUGGESTED READINGS

Kernberg O. F. (1984). *Severe Personality Disorders: Psychotherapeutic Strategies*, pp. 249–253. New Haven, CT: Yale University Press.

Ticho, E. (1972). The effects of the psychoanalyst's personality on the treatment. *Psychoanalytic Forum* 4:221–247.

Waelder, R. (1936). The principle of multiple function: observations on overdetermination. *Psychoanalytic Quarterly* 5:45–62.

63. What is meant by the *initial contract*?

Before embarking on intensive psychotherapy, it is essential that the therapist and patient agree on the goals of therapy, its method, the roles and responsibilities of each participant, and the limits of their responsibilities. Well-motivated individuals with minimal ego impairment pose little difficulty in comprehending and accepting such guidelines. Others (especially borderline patients) require more explicit directions and the establishment of a firmer initial contract. Such a contract has two components. One consists of standard responsibilities (e.g., schedule, payment, and open communication) for both the patient and therapist that are integral to any psychoanalytic psychotherapy. The other involves specific issues (e.g., self-mutilation, anorexia, irregular attendance of sessions) arising from each patient's individual psychopathology. The main purpose of the contract is to safeguard the therapist's technical neutrality and to protect the intrapsychic exploratory work from the behavioral attacks (seductive or aggressive) of the patient. It defines the therapeutic framework and outlines the least restrictive set of conditions to protect its boundaries. The contract also alerts the patient regarding anticipated patterns of his sabotaging the treatment, and provides an anchoring point for the therapist's self-monitoring of his own inclinations to deviate from the initial contract. By accomplishing this, the participants create a lesser likelihood of patient dropout. While it might appear rigid, the contract is not aimed to suppress the intense intrapsychic life of the patient but to allow that intensity to evolve safely. Three other aspects of the initial contract need to be kept in mind:

(1) The contract is not a unilateral proclamation but the result of a collaborative effort between the patient and the therapist. The therapist must not only explicitly state the expected roles and responsibilities of both parties but must also carefully evaluate the patient's understanding of what was said and the patient's re-

sponse to it. The patient might refuse to hear, act bored, or blatantly deny what is being said. More often, the patient seems to have heard the words but not thought about their implications. Willingness to accept exists on a continuum ranging from outright refusal through substituting one's own conditions to a "yes, but" sort of response. The therapist must decide whether to accept the patient's response as adequate for beginning therapy or to explore further the implicit or explicit opposition to the contract.

(2) The contract establishes the necessary conditions of the therapy, not of the therapist. The patient who fails to understand this may feel capriciously dealt with by the therapist. The therapist who fails to understand this is vulnerable to abdicate aspects of the contract (e.g., required frequency of sessions) in the face of the patient's objections. Or, the therapist might ignore the patient's objections, sidestep confrontation, and enter into a pseudoagreement, a harbinger of failed treatment.

(3) The value of the contract as a reference point persists throughout the treatment, even during its advanced stages. Yeomans and colleagues (1992), who have described in great detail a contract-based approach to treating borderline patients, emphasize that the therapist working in this fashion repeatedly refers back to the treatment contract. "As soon as there is evidence that the patient is deviating from one of the parameters, the therapist focuses on that and reminds the patient of what the treatment requires. He does not overlook it or let it slip by, but rather addresses it as a crucial matter" (p. 178).

SUGGESTED READINGS

Kernberg, O. F., Selzer, M. A., Koenigsberg, H. W., et al. (1989). *Psychodynamic Psychotherapy of Borderline Patients.* New York: Basic Books.

Selzer, M. A., Koenigsberg, H. W., and Kernberg, O. F. (1987). The initial contract in the treatment of borderline patients. *American Journal of Psychiatry* 144:927–930.

Yeomans, F. E., Selzer, M. A., and Clarkin, J. F. (1992). *Treating the Borderline Patient: A Contract Based Approach.* New York: Basic Books.

64. How does the concept of *holding environment* contribute to the therapeutic armamentarium?

The term *holding environment* was coined by Donald Winnicott in 1960. He used it in connection with the ordinary function of a mother holding her infant. Holding in this context meant "not only the actual physical holding of the infant, but also the total environmental provision (p. 43). Winnicott emphasized that first and foremost the holding environment must meet physiological needs and be reliable. Its reliability, however, is not in a machine-like predictability but in its remaining empathically attuned to the child's needs, which vary from moment to moment. The holding environment does not abandon, nor does it impinge. It facilitates growth. Moreover, it extends beyond the infantile period to the broader caretaking functions of the parents in relation to the older child.

Winnicott believed that the psychotherapeutic situation should be a holding environment. It should provide safety, security, and containment of strong affects, while helping the patient's growth potential to be reactivated. Winnicott's notions in this regard have been further developed by Harry Guntrip, Masud Khan, and (more recently) Patrick Casement in England, and Arnold Modell, Gerald Adler, and Roger Lewin and Clarence Schulz in the United States. Discernible in these contributions is the impact of the holding environment concept on at least four aspects of psychoanalytic and psychotherapeutic technique.

(1) *Physical aspects*: A therapist mindful of the holding environment would have a certain attitude toward the physical environment in which his and the patient's mutual work is to be carried out. In setting up his office, he would avoid both ostentatiousness and asceticism. He would make his office comfortable, noise free, and authentic, without undue self-revelation. He would avoid frequently altering the decor and safeguard the physical integrity of this environment.

(2) *Psychological atmosphere*: The holding environment concept also translates into the therapist's providing an ambience of trust, emotional safety, and acceptance. The therapist is there "primarily for the patient and not for his own [benefit]; he does not retaliate, and he does at times have a better grasp of the patient's inner reality than does the patient himself and therefore may clarify what is bewildering and confusing" (Modell 1976, p. 29).

(3) *Environmental interpretations*: The concept of the holding environment might also guide the content of interpretations. Interpreting the patient's experience and use of the therapist as a much-needed environmental provision (in contrast to a specific human object) is what I have in mind here. An example of such environmental interpretations is the following. To a patient who was profoundly upset about an upcoming separation, I once said: "It seems to me that sometimes I am like an ocean to you, in which you swim freely like a fish; at other times, I am like a jar and you the water nicely contained in it. In either case, my leaving feels profoundly threatening to you, since it is like an ocean drying up for a fish or a jar breaking for the water in it." This interpretation likened the transference relationship to an environment rather than to a specific person and in so doing relied heavily on the concept of the holding environment.

(4) *Interpreting fantasies about the holding function*: The holding and caretaking functions of the therapist might themselves become the foci of the patient's fantasies. These require interpretative resolution of their own, especially toward the later phases of the treatment.

SUGGESTED READINGS

Lewin, R., and Schulz, C. (1992). *Losing and Fusing: Borderline Transitional Object and Self Relations*, pp. 111–178. Northvale, NJ: Jason Aronson.

Modell, A. (1976). The holding environment and the therapeutic action of psychoanalysis. *Journal of the American Psychoanalytic Association* 24:285–307.

Winnicott, D. W. (1960). Ego distortion in terms of true and false. In *The Maturational Processes and the Facilitating Environment*, pp. 140–152. New York: International Universities Press.

65. Do individuals with severe personality disorders tend to develop certain specific transferences?

Although each individual patient is unique, it is true that those with severe personality disorders do tend to develop certain specific type of transferences. The fundamental themes of these transferences are (1) a search for an all-good object, often felt as a pressing and unquestionable need either for *mirroring* one's self experience (thus rendering it authentic and valuable) or for *idealizing* an other in order to bask in the warmth of such borrowed strength; and (2) a revenge motif, involving an all-bad object representation and permitting guilt-free attacks on the therapeutic setting. The former transference propensity, besides giving rise to a need for being mirrored, manifests as sustained idealization (and the related attitude of perpetual waiting for the analyst to magically solve all problems) in narcissistic and schizoid patients, defensive and superficial collusion in as-if and infantile patients, and worshiping awe coupled with hungry pleading for love and guidance in borderline patients. The latter transference propensity manifests as cold and haughty devaluation of the therapist in narcissistic and paranoid patients, outbursts of contempt and impulsive destructive actions in borderline patients, and a pouting withdrawal into futility in schizoid patients.

The basically contradictory nature of these transferences sooner or later leads to both idealization and devaluation of the therapist. In the more ego-impaired patients, the two attitudes are consciously, though alternately, experienced with comparable conviction. In better integrated patients, such fluctuations are mild, and/or one side is experienced in relation to the therapist and the other in relation to someone outside the treatment, and/or one attitude is emphatically professed and felt while the behavior gives evidence to the contrary.

Inevitably, there is an intermingling of oedipal themes in the two transferences. The persistence of infantile omnipotence seriously interferes with the establishment of an incest barrier; the longing for an all-good symbiotic mother is frequently condensed with desires for oedipal gratification. The result is a malignant erotic transference with the patient insistently seeking sex and/or marriage with the therapist/analyst. At the same time, the patient shows evidence that the much-desired gratification is also related in the patient's mind (albeit unconsciously) with preoedipal hate and oedipal guilt. Consequently, the seeming entitlement the patient feels is tacitly colored by its opposite, leading to much inner confusion.

While such idealizing, devaluing, and desperately controlling erotic transferences are easily recognizable, there is a more subtle form of transference displayed by certain narcissistic and schizoid patients and by some individuals who have been markedly impinged upon, intruded on, and abused as children. This involves the patient's appearing to be totally uninvolved with the therapist over a sustained length of time. Through hesitant or tenacious silence, superficial and externally focused associations, even verbal excess, the patient avoids any allusions to transference and creates a firm barrier between himself and the therapist. In such a *cocoon phase* (Modell 1976), the patient is largely in a state of psychic incubation, waiting to accumulate enough benevolent experience to be able to truly relate to the therapist.

SUGGESTED READINGS

Kernberg, O. F. (1975). Borderline personality organization. In *Borderline Conditions and Pathological Narcissism*, pp. 1–47. New York: Jason Aronson.

Kohut, H. (1971). *The Analysis of the Self*, pp. 37–56, 105–142. New York: International Universities Press.

Modell, H. (1976). The holding environment and the therapeutic action of psychoanalysis. *Journal of the American Psychoanalytic Association* 24:285–307.

66. What is *erotized transference*?

In his paper "Observations on Transference Love," Freud (1915) described the development of tender and romantic feelings in the patient toward the therapist. He emphasized the value of a tolerant, dispassionate, and yet skeptical attitude if the "infantile roots" (p. 166) of such love are to be traced. Most patients are amenable to this line of investigation. However, Freud acknowledged that there is "one class of women with whom this attempt to preserve the erotic transference for the purposes of analytic work without satisfying it will not succeed. These are women of elemental passionateness who tolerate no surrogates. They are children of nature who refuse to accept the psychical in place of the material" (pp. 166–167).

This latter attitude received a comprehensive description by Harold Blum (1973) under the rubric of *erotized transference*. Blum emphasized that underlying such erotic demands are intense object hunger, defective self- and object constancy, fears of depletion and engulfment, infantile omnipotence, and much sadomasochism. A relentless pursuit of the all-good mother of symbiosis has become condensed with positive oedipal strivings. The parallel amalgamation of the bad-mother representation with the oedipal rival creates vengeful hostility, which is often split-off, denied, displaced onto others, or enacted in a contradictory but unassimilated manner toward the analyst. Condensation of the good-mother representation with that of the desired oedipal partner gives rise to intense longings experienced as unquestionable needs. However, "the pre-eminent oral insatiability, the vulnerability to disappointment and detachment, the underlying sadomasochism soon become apparent" (Blum 1973, p. 69).

Four aspects of such *malignant erotic transference* (Akhtar 1994) are: (1) predominance of hostility over love in the seemingly erotic overtures, (2) intense coercion of the analyst to indulge in actions, (3) inconsolability in the face of the analyst's depriving stance, and (4) the absence of erotic counterresonance in the analyst, who experiences the patient's demands as intrusive, controlling, and hostile. In the throes of such transference, the patient can become convinced the analyst should (or will) actually consummate their relationship and marry her. This shows a beginning loss of reality testing and is a cause for alarm. Conversely, in patients who, in a near-psychotic version of such transference, are insistent that the analyst marry them right now, a movement toward waiting for that to happen implies the dawning capacity to tolerate postponement of desire. This might constitute the first evidence of a strengthened capacity to mourn and renounce omnipotent claims on reality.

The (possibly) greater frequency of malignant erotic transference in women seems to have several explanations: (1) more intense reproaches in the female child toward the mother, (2) the extra burden on the female child's ego to mourn the "loss" of the penis, and (3) the actual experience, in the background of many such patients, of having been "picked up" by their fathers after being "dropped" by their mothers. This, while saving the child from a schizoid or suicidal breakdown, robs her of a fundamental prototype of mourning; instead, she learns that what is lost (all-good mother) can indeed be found (overindulgent father). The fact that such rescues are usually quite instinctualized contributes to sadomasochistic sexual fantasies and a perverse defiance of oedipal limits in later adult life.

SUGGESTED READINGS

Akhtar, S. (1994). Object constancy and adult psychopathology. *International Journal of Psycho-Analysis* 75:441–455.

Blum, H. P. (1973). The concept of erotized transference. *Journal of the American Psychoanalytic Association* 21:61–76.

Freud, S. (1915). Observations on transference-love. *Standard Edition* 12:155–171.

67. What is *mirror transference*?

Although the metaphor of the mirror has been used by various psychoanalytic theorists (e.g., Winnicott, Lacan, Mahler) in overlapping but distinguishable ways, the concept of *mirror transference* owes its origin to Heinz Kohut (1971). Familiarity with his developmental hypotheses regarding narcissistic personality is necessary for one to understand this concept properly.

Kohut proposed that the *grandiose self* is a psychic structure that reflects the infantile phase in which the child attempts to save this primary narcissism by concentrating power and perfection upon the self and by turning away from the external world. Over the course of optimal development, the grandiose self is increasingly subsumed within the reality ego. For this to occur, adequate reflection ("mirroring") of the growing child's healthy narcissism is necessary. When this is deficient, the grandiose self becomes separated from the reality ego and is repressed. *The activation of this repressed grandiose self during analyses of individuals with narcissistic personality disorder constitutes the essence of mirror transference.*

Kohut outlined three types of mirror transferences: (1) *Merger type*: In this transference, the patient experiences the analyst as an extension of his grandiose self. It is as if the analyst were a part of him with no mind of his own. The patient expects "unquestioned dominance over him . . . [while] the analyst experiences this relationship in general as oppressive" (Kohut 1971, p. 115); (2) *Alter-ego type*: This manifests in the patient's experience of the narcissistically invested object as being similar to his grandiose self. The patient feels that the analyst is very much like him, that is, they are psychological twins. The patient dreams and fantasizes about a relationship with such a "twin"; and (3) *The true mirror transference*: Here the patient does experience the analyst as a separate person but one whose significance is restricted to reflecting the patient's grandiose self. Such mirror transference is the therapeutic reinstatement of that normal phase of the development of the grandiose self in which the gleam in the mother's eye, which mirrors the child's exhibitionistic display and other forms of maternal participation in and response to the child's narcissistic-exhibitionistic enjoyment confirm the child's self-esteem and, by a gradually increasing selectivity of these responses, begin to channel it into realistic directions. [p. 116]

Kohut's technical approach to these transferences consists of (1) interpreting the defensive denials of demands for mirroring, (2) bringing the central sector of the personality to acknowledge the split-off grandiosity, (3) not pointing out the unrealistic nature of the patient's expectations, (4) maintaining an attitude of acceptance, and (5) demonstrating to the patient that his demands are valid, given the context of an early developmental phase being revived in transference. A "slow process is thus initiated which leads — by almost imperceptible steps, and often without any specific explanations from the side of the analyst — to the integration of the grandiose self into the structure of the reality ego" (p. 176).

While his descriptions of these transferences are widely accepted, Kohut's technical approach remains controversial. It is especially questioned by those theorists (e.g., Kernberg and his exponents) who see the grandiose self as a pathological structure to begin with. Their approach to such transferences, in contrast, focuses upon their defensive functions against rage and hatred toward the analyst.

SUGGESTED READINGS

Akhtar, S. (1989). Kohut and Kernberg: a critical comparison. In *Self Psychology: Comparisons and Contrasts*, ed. D. W. Detrick and S. P. Detrick, pp. 329–362. Hillsdale, NJ: Analytic Press.

Kohut, H. (1971). *The Analysis of the Self*, pp. 105–196. New York: International Universities Press.

———— (1977). *Restoration of the Self*. New York: International Universities Press.

68. What is *idealizing transference*?

The term *idealizing transference* was introduced into the psycho-analytic literature by Heinz Kohut in 1971. Familiarity with his developmental hypotheses regarding narcissistic personality is necessary for one to understand this concept properly.

Kohut proposed that the child's primary narcissism is inevitably injured, and to compensate for this disturbance, the child employs two maneuvers. One involves an insistent refocusing of narcissism upon the self (the grandiose self) and the other involves attributing perfection to parents (the idealized parent imago) and then basking in the reflection of that glory. Under normal circumstances, this idealization is gradually withdrawn. The child's growing capacity to see the parents in a true light and the empathic parents' gradual revelation of their shortcomings facilitate such de-idealization. Disappointment with parents (especially the same sex parent) during the oedipal phase also contributes to a diminishing idealization of them. Instead, such idealization is invested in the superego, which acquires a "super" or exalted position vis-à-vis the ego.

This normal course of events is interrupted if the child suffers a traumatic loss of the idealized object or a severe and sudden disappointment in it. A parent's "unempathic modesty" (Kohut 1971, p. 43) might also frustrate the child's phase-specific need to idealize him or her. Under these circumstances, the child fails to accomplish the gradual de-idealization of the parents necessary for strengthening his own psychic structure. Instead, the child remains fixated upon an archaic selfobject (i.e., the idealized parent imago) for self-esteem regulation and approval.

The activation of this *idealized parent imago* during the treatment of narcissistic individuals is termed *idealizing transference*. In Kohut's (1971) own words, idealizing transference is

the revival during psychoanalysis of . . . the state in which, after being exposed to the disturbance of the psychological equilibrium of primary narcissism, the psyche saves a part of the lost experience of global narcissistic perfection by assigning it to an archaic, rudimentary (transitional) self-object, the idealized parent imago [p. 37]

Kohut described two types of idealizing transference. The first is based on the activation of the archaic state in which the idealized mother imago is almost completely merged with the self. The second emanates from later developmental phases where a traumatic disappointment in parents has led to impaired de-idealization of them and insufficient idealization of the superego. Individuals of the latter type are forever attempting to achieve a union with an idealized object. They attempt to do the same in the treatment situation. They view the analyst as omnipotent and feel whole, safe, and strong as long as they can maintain such idealization. They respond to disappointments in the analyst by denial or by despondency and rage. Indeed, it is the repeated occurrence of such disruptions and their affirmative-reconstructive handling that, in the view of Kohut and his followers, leads to transmuting internalization of idealization and an enhanced ability to regulate self-esteem.

While the phenomena described by Kohut are widely accepted, many alternate viewpoints exist regarding their technical handling. For instance, Kernberg, who views such idealization as a defense against transference hatred of the analyst, recommends a sharper focus on the negative transference in the treatment of these patients.

SUGGESTED READINGS

Akhtar, S. (1989). Kohut and Kernberg: a critical comparison. In *Self Psychology: Comparisons and Contrasts,* ed. D. W. Detrick and S. P. Detrick, pp. 329–362. Hillsdale, NJ: Analytic Press.

Kohut, H. (1971). *The Analysis of the Self*, pp. 37–101. New York: International Universities Press.

Kohut, H., and Wolf, E. (1978). The disorders of the self and their treatment: an outline. *International Journal of Psycho-Analysis* 59:413–425.

69. How do the concepts of *conflict* and *deficit* inform psychotherapeutic and psychoanalytic technique?

Psychoanalytic theory has traditionally viewed psychopathology in terms of intrapsychic *conflict*. Though concepts such as "partially internalized conflicts" or "object relations conflicts" have existed on the sidelines, the emphasis of theory has been upon structural conflicts, that is, those involving an opposition among id, ego, and superego. This model requires (1) that there be a clear differentiation between self- and object representations and that these structures have a certain degree of stability (self- and object constancy), (2) that the three psychic structures (id, ego, and superego) be clearly demarcated from each other, and (3) that repression should have replaced splitting as the main ego mechanism of defense.

Individuals with severe personality disorders are not at this psychostructural level. At least, they are not at this level most of the time and in most aspects of their characterological make up. Certain aspects of their psychopathology do not appear related to forces opposing each other. Instead, they seem related to intrasystemic failures or *deficits*, such as defective object constancy, ego-weakness, incapacity for emotional relating to objects and so on. However, such derivatives of deficit are intricately interwoven with conflict-based issues. They cannot be surgically separated. There is no personality disorder entirely organized around deficit, only ones with deficit-related areas.

The technical relevance of this distinction comes from the fact that *conflict-related psychopathology* implies intentionality (i.e., the capacity to conceive of oneself as an agent of one's thoughts, aims, and actions) and hence the need to disguise one's unacceptable wishes. Such pathology is essentially one of concealed meaning. Its treatment is aimed at unmasking and deciphering these covert messages. Skeptical listening is the mainstay of the analyst's receptivity and interpretive interventions are the chief tool of his activity. *The deficit-related psychopathology*, in contrast, lacks intentionality.

> Due either to overwhelming stimulation, or inadequate stimulation or to deprivation, the ego has been injured at a time when the ability to represent cause and effect and the ability to experience the self as a strategic centre have not yet been developed. . . . Thus, in pathology based on deficit, it is not a matter of defending oneself against anxiety connected with bad intentions, e.g., forbidden object-directed needs, fantasies, and feelings, as is the case in conflict. What is defended against is primarily anxiety of fragmentation, i.e., losing one's own feeling of identity. [Killingmo 1989, p. 67]

The therapeutic endeavor in such circumstances is not a search for hidden meaning but "rather to assist the ego in expressing *meaning in itself*. It is not a matter of finding something else, but to feel that something has the quality of being (Killingmo 1989, p. 67; Killingmo's emphasis). A more credulous form of listening is required here, though without the sacrifice of the analytic attitude altogether. Also, interventions made are not of the interpretive, unmasking kind but of the "affirmative" variety, which accept, objectify and justify the patient's experience. To be sure, ideal technique requires that the therapist oscillate between the investigative-interpretive mode and the credulous-affirmative mode as the patient's transference shifts from the hesitant, multilayered conflict-related material to the insistent, desperate, and relatively simple deficit-based material.

SUGGESTED READINGS

Dorpat, T. L. (1976). Structural conflict and object relations conflict. *Journal of the American Psychoanalytic Association* 24:855–874.

Killingmo, B. (1989). Conflict and deficit: implications for technique. *International Journal of Psycho-Analysis* 70:65–79.

Schaffer, R. (1963). *The Analytic Attitude*. New York: Basic Books.

70. Are there special techniques for interpreting splitting?

Individuals with severe personality disorders lack object constancy and frequently resort to the defense mechanism of splitting. Faced with the reactivation of unmet anaclitic longings of childhood, they are given to idealize the therapist. Faced with the reactivation of rage and hatred directed at internalized parental figures, they are given to devalue the therapist. Their ego is weak and cannot contain such intense ambivalence. Consequently, they oscillate between the two contradictory attitudes, each occurring in its own right, besides being employed as a defense against its affectively opposite counterpart. The self-estimations of these patients shift abruptly, and so do their transferences. According to Kernberg (1975), psychotherapeutic intervention with them "is not a matter of searching for unconscious, repressed material, but *bridging and integrating* what appear on the surface to be two or more emotionally independent, but alternately active ego states" (p. 96; italics added). But how is this "bridging" and "integrating" to be done? And, could the reasons for one or the other side of the split transference being active at a certain time be unconscious? Similarly, could the fact of their deployment as defenses (both against each other as well as against higher level, oedipal-type issues) be unconscious? It seems that further explication of the "bridging" interventions is needed and so is a greater attention to what indeed might be unconscious aspects of the use of splitting. Guided in this fashion by Kernberg's ideas, but expanding upon them, I have delineated three technical aspects of significance in addressing the splitting defense.

(1) *Conceptual stance*: The analyst must have a firm allegiance to the "principle of multiple function" (Waelder 1936). This would allow him to accommodate various perspectives on the patient's pathology and reduce his vulnerability to the simplistic either/or conceptualizations regarding love and hate, drive and defense, deficit and conflict, oedipal and preoedipal, and so on. It

might also help the therapist to temper his countertransference; he should remember that the poignant, rescue-evoking patient and the contemptuous, hate-evoking patient are one and the same individual at all times.

(2) *Bridging interventions*: An effort should be made to undo the psychic compartmentalization caused by splitting. The therapist must retain the patient's contradictory self- and object representations in mind since the patient has a tendency to affectively "forget" one or the other extreme of his experience. The therapist's interventions, for a long time, might be usefully tempered by his display that he, at least, has not "forgotten" the opposite transference configuration (for example: "This hate that, despite your parallel love, you feel for me at this time is . . ." or "I know you like me a lot, though of course at other times you feel quite differently about me" etc.). Focus on negative transference should be accompanied by a gentle verbal reminder of the patient's love for the therapist and elucidation of the latter should be accompanied by a mild remark regarding the patient's hostility.

(3) *Interpretive interventions*: Attention should also be paid to the unconscious reasons for the defensive activation of splitting and the unconscious use of one feeling state to defend against the anxiety about the other (e.g., hatred as a defense against love, and vice versa).

SUGGESTED READINGS

Akhtar, S. (1994). Object constancy and adult psychopathology. *International Journal of Psycho-Analysis* 75:441–455.

Kernberg, O. F. (1975). *Borderline Conditions and Pathological Narcissism*, pp. 94–96. New York: Jason Aronson.

Waelder, R. (1936). The principle of multiple function. *Psychoanalytic Quarterly* 5:45–62.

71. How should the therapist respond to protracted silences of the patient?

The therapist's response to protracted silences of the patient depends on his understanding of their nature. *If he views such silences as representing the overall character style of the patient,* then he should begin by gently reminding the patient of the necessity to verbalize his thoughts and feelings. He should make empathic remarks regarding the unusual nature of the therapeutic situation, which requires the patient to talk, something the latter has not been used to. The therapist might also attempt to explore situations in the patient's past in which talking was needed but seemed immensely difficult. Failing to engage the patient in a verbal exchange, the therapist should reevaluate his choice of treatment modality. After all, poor capacity to verbalize thoughts and feelings, regardless of its reason, is a contraindication to psychoanalytic psychotherapy and psychoanalysis. While reflecting on how this was missed during evaluation, the therapist should consider (and discuss with the patient) alternate therapeutic strategies that either require less expressiveness (pharmacotherapy and/or supportive psychotherapy) or can better confront deeply ingrained character resistances (group therapy).

If, on the other hand, the therapist feels that such silences are specific to the treatment situation, then he should proceed differently. His interventions should be guided by the awareness that such silences have many potential causes. These include: (1) *Resistance*: If the therapist feels that the patient's silence is due to anxiety about revealing his feelings and fantasies, then his interventions should aim to relieve this tension ("It seems that you want me to reassure you that I can peacefully listen to whatever you might say"; "You seem afraid of my reaction—and perhaps even your own—to what might emerge were you to talk openly," etc.). (2) *Transference of defense*: If the therapist discerns that the patient's silence is an unconscious replication of his childhood attempts at hiding feelings from his parents, then this defense transference needs to be interpreted as such before pursuing what is hidden underneath the silence. (3) *Silence as enactment*: The patient's long silences might be acted-out, unconscious fantasies. These fantasies vary greatly and involve identification with a stubbornly silent parent (with the therapist now in the child/patient's role), playing possum to avoid a murderous assault from the therapist (equated with a hateful parent), and so on. (4) *Silence as an assault on the therapist/therapy*: Envy of the therapist's psychic autonomy and resourcefulness might lead the patient to angrily withhold information. The resulting silences might also seek to provoke the therapist's rage so that the patient does not have to own up to his transference hatred; and finally (5) *Silence as the moment of hesitation*: Often the patient, like an infant taking a toy from a stranger, hesitates a few moments before beginning to talk. In patients with problems of trust, such hesitation is more persistent. Their silences should not be punctured by interventions but should simply be tolerated. One can goad such a patient into talking but the response would be inauthentic. Clearly, this list does not exhast the causes of long silences nor does it imply that these causes are mutually exclusive.

The technical approach of the therapist should ultimately depend on his understanding of a particular silence at a particular moment in the light of both the patient's reported history and the unfolding transference–countertransference dialogue.

SUGGESTED READINGS

Arlow, J. (1961). Silence and the theory of technique. *Journal of the American Psychoanalytic Association* 9:44–55.

Kernberg, O. F., Selzer, M. A., Koenigsberg, H. W., et al. (1990). *Psychodynamic Psychotherapy of Borderline Patients*. New York: Basic Books.

Khan, M. M. R. (1963). Silence as communication. In *The Privacy of the Self*, pp. 168–180. New York: International Universities Press, 1973.

72. Does the interpretive process also refer to nonverbal communications of the patient?

Although psychoanalysis and psychoanalytic psychotherapy are basically "talking cures," the fact remains that the talking in them also involves forms of communication other than verbalized speech. For instance, the motor vocabulary of play constitutes a significant part of communication in child analysis or psychotherapy. In the treatment of adults, however, the role of nonverbal communication has received only gradual and belated recognition. Freud noted it, of course, but his emphasis remained upon the resistance aspects of various behaviors during the treatment situation. "Repeating" (i.e, the enactment of an early memory or fantasy) was viewed as an impediment to remembering and working through.

The communicative (rather than resistant) aspects of nonverbal behavior began to be addressed in the views of Wilhelm Reich on *character armour*, Felix Deutsch on *analytic posturology*, and Meyer Zeligs on *acting in*. This line of investigation received further impetus from the growing analytic attention, over the last three decades, to patients with more severe ego disturbances than the traditional neurotic patient. More recently, Theodore Jacobs and James McLaughlin have made highly significant contributions that reveal how postural changes and bodily movements (both of the patient and the therapist) during the treatment hour can deepen the empathic understanding of the patient.

While such nonverbal communications occur during the treatment of all patients, they acquire a greater significance in the treatment of those with severe character pathology. Such individuals live out their problem of object constancy rather than talking about it and reflecting upon what is said. They behave rather than recall. For them, object constancy is externally represented by any form of ideation that serves to maintain the contact with the therapist. Their regressive struggle to recapture the symbiotic bond with their mothers defies customary discourse. Fantasy elaboration is meager and the raw data pointing to early ego impairment tends to be affectual rather than verbal. The residues of such preverbal issues, however, lie unabated under the adult persona, and are often discernible only through the "behavioral dance and somatic music" (McLaughlin 1992, p. 151) of the patient, which reverberates at its loudest in the analyst's counter-transference. Examples of such behaviors include a patient's furtively touching his mouth again and again while being silent, or a sitting-up patient's tenacious avoidance of eye contact, or a patient's looking intensely at the therapist right before leaving the office, and so forth.

Clearly such behaviors are multiply determined. They have both resistance and communicative values. They might contain conflicts, memories, defenses, and developmental needs from various levels. The important question is whether guidelines for pointing out such behaviors exist. While no hard and fast rule can be made, and clinical intuition must remain the final arbiter, it seems advisable to address (point out, ask for patient's associations, interpret, etc.) such behaviors only when (1) the behavior is striking or bizarre, (2) the verbal content has dried up or is truly intellectualized, (3) the verbal content can be linked up with the behavior in question (e.g., the patient who looks intently at the therapist at each session's end and is talking of his pain at separations), and (4) the behavior is disruptive to the treatment framework.

SUGGESTED READINGS

Freud, S. (1914). Remembering, repeating, and working through (further recommendations on the technique of psychoanalysis — II). *Standard Edition* 12:145–156.

Lilleskov, R. K. (1977). Panel report: Nonverbal aspects of child and adult psychoanalysis. *Journal of the American Psychoanalytic Association* 25:693–705.

McLaughlin, J. T. (1992). Nonverbal behaviors in the analytic situation: the search for meaning in nonverbal cues. In *When the Body Speaks: Psychological Meanings in Kinetic Clues*, pp. 131–162, ed. S. Kramer and S. Akhtar. Northvale, NJ: Jason Aronson.

73. How does the distinction between *needs* and *wishes* affect therapeutic technique?

Classical psychoanalysis and the psychotherapies derived from it regard the patient's demands as disguised derivatives of unconscious wishes. Such skepticism prompts an interpretive stance toward these requests. The therapist points out their resistance value, indicates their evocative functions, or invites the patient to join him in a mutual attempt at discovering their actual meanings. The therapist's stance is one of abstinence, curiosity, and interpretation.

A minority opinion within psychoanalysis, however, holds that just as there are physical needs (e.g., food) there are psychological needs (e.g., being understood and affirmed, causality, vitality) which, unlike wishes, are neither experience bound nor subject to repression. This viewpoint allows for the possibility that the patient's demands might be based on genuine developmental needs. Such orientation impels the therapist to take an attitude of credulousness, empathy, affirmation, and, occasionally, even gratification of the patient's needs.

The *distinction between needs and wishes* is not easily made on a clinical level. In the course of development, needs and wishes become condensed and alter each other in the process. Moreover, a person driven by entitlement experiences wishes as pressing needs, and one with an ascetic bent denounces needs as mere wishes. Also, unmet developmental needs result not in psychic holes but in powerful compensatory structures. A therapist cannot simply fill such lacunae by kindness. The patient's rage over unmet needs, and guilt over this rage, are also activated in the transference, combatting any attempts at solace. What is to be done?

Here is a situation that addresses this question. The therapist is about to leave for vacation. The patient insists that he *needs* to know where the therapist is going, and is beside himself. The therapist's inviting him to explore the meanings of this demand holds no appeal. Now, should the therapist tell the patient his destination? If one views the patient as being in a symbiotic-like oneness with the therapist, where self- and object boundaries have merged and the separation is indeed tearing the patient apart, then one might see a need element in this request. However, if one sees this request as an angry refusal to permit a love object its autonomy, or a disguised intrusion into the privacy of the parental couple, then one might see wish elements in it. The former stance tilts the balance toward gratification (providing ego support), the latter toward deprivation (restraining an id upsurge). The situation, however, is complex because such a demand generally has both need and wish elements. Therefore, in gratifying or frustrating one, something is also done to the other. Whatever one does has advantages and disadvantages. For instance, in letting the patient know where one is going, one may enhance the patient's sense of safety and diminish his pain. However, it may also disappoint him since it frustrates his contradictory need for the therapist to be able to withstand his assaults. It might also stir up guilt in the patient because it has satisfied a prohibited wish involving a primal scene fantasy. Of course, the therapist's doing the opposite would have its own pros and cons. The therapist should also remember that (1) ego support and id gratification are different, even if not easily separable; (2) transference is affected by both gratification and deprivation; (3) the intervention chosen should match the patient's ego strength and help preserve the treatment alliance; and (4) the effects of one's intervention should be looked for and handled in an interpretive manner.

SUGGESTED READINGS

Akhtar, S. (1994). Needs, disruptions, and the return of ego instincts. In *Mahler and Kohut: Perspectives on Development, Psychopathology and Treatment*, eds. S. Kramer and S. Akhtar, pp. 97–115. Northvale, NJ: Jason Aronson.

Casement, P. (1991). *Learning from the Patient*, pp. 273–292. New York: Guilford.

Wolf, E. (1994). Selfobject experiences: development, psychopathology, treatment. In *Mahler and Kohut: Perspectives on Development, Psychopathology and Treatment*, eds. S. Kramer and S. Akhtar, pp. 65–96. Northvale, NJ: Jason Aronson.

74. What are *affirmative interventions*?

The term *affirmative interventions* was introduced into the psychoanalytic literature by Bjorn Killingmo in 1989. Killingmo stated that the psychological essence of the concept is formed by four elements listed by Cissna and Sieburg (1981). These are (1) the element of existence, (2) the element of relating, (3) the element of worth, and (4) the element of validity of experience. Killingmo further noted that interventions containing these elements are distinct from traditional interpretive interventions aimed at deciphering and unmasking hidden meanings. Affirmative interventions, in contrast, are aimed at establishing plausibility that the patient's experience is indeed valid and meaningful. Interpretive interventions are primarily relevant in the dynamic context of intrapsychic conflict, affirmative interventions in the dynamic context of structural deficit.

Killingmo acknowledged that many similar concepts, for example, "empathic reconstructive-interpretation" (Ornstein and Ornstein 1980) had existed before. However, he suggested that these terms could be subsumed under his concept of *affirmative intervention*, which would also include the holding and containing notions of Winnicott and Bion respectively. True, these latter concepts appear broader since they refer to more implicit aspects of the analyst's behavior. Nevertheless, they, too, are aimed at enhancing the subjective quality of meaningfulness. "Certainly the affirmative quality is not dependent on words. It may well be conveyed by saying nothing in the right way" (Killingmo 1989, p. 68).

To reiterate, affirmative interventions are not directed at revealing meaning. They are directed at establishing the existence of meaning. On a pragmatic level, verbally offered affirmative interventions are comprised of (1) an *objectifying element* that conveys the sense to the patient that the therapist can feel what it is to be in the patient's shoes (e.g., "Your tense silence, distraught appearance, and avoidance of me all tell me that you are profoundly upset and find the situation unbearably painful"). This renders the affective experience of the patient less private. "It becomes something that has shape, can be shared with an other and eventually be put into words" (Killingmo 1989, p. 73); (2) a *justifying element* that introduces a cause-and-effect relation, thus placing the patient's feeling state in the context of a reasonable sequence of events (e.g., "No wonder you feel so upset at my announcing my vacation since you feel desperately lost without me and, on top of that, feel so helplessly excluded from my decisions in this regard"); and (3) *an accepting element* that imparts an historical context to the current distress by including the mention of similar experiences from the patient's past (e.g., "I know that my leaving hurts you deeply because it reminds you of the time when you were 4 or 5 years old and your parents would go away for weeks at a time, leaving you pining for them").

It should be emphasized that such interventions do not require any special indulgence in the patient and can be made while maintaining a neutral position. They strengthen the therapeutic alliance and enhance the recognition of the emotional turmoil as a transference reaction, which thus becomes amenable to more traditional interpretive intervention.

SUGGESTED READINGS

Cissna, K. N. L. and Sieburg, E. (1981). Patterns of confirmation and disconfirmation. In *Rigor and Imagination: Essays from the Legacy of Gregory Bateson*, ed. C. Wilder-Mott and J. H. Weakland. New York: Praeger.

Killingmo, B. (1989). Conflict and deficit: implications for technique. *International Journal of Psycho-Analysis* 70:65–79.

Ornstein, P. H. and Ornstein, A. (1980). Formulating interpretations in clinical psychoanalysis. *International Journal of Psycho-Analysis* 61:203–211.

75. What is *emotional flooding* and how might the therapist respond to it?

In 1976, Vamık Volkan categorized the nature of patients' emotionality during treatment sessions into three types (while acknowledging the frequent occurrence of mixed forms). These three types were: (1) abreaction, (2) affectualization, and (3) emotional flooding. *Abreaction*, originally considered curative in its own right, is now largely thought of as establishing conviction in the patient as to the "actuality" of his repressed impulses and object-related fantasies. Volkan emphasized that an emotional storm during the therapeutic process is an abreaction when the patient can himself (or readily with help from the analyst) see the connection between the emotional, ideational, and behavioral realms. The patient's observing ego is not overwhelmed by emotion. *Affectualization*, originally described by Edward Bibring and colleagues (1961), is a characterological overemphasis on the emotional aspects of an issue in order to avoid a deeper, rational understanding of it. Such emotionality is an ego defense that becomes incorporated as a character trait in some individuals.

Emotional flooding is distinct from both abreaction and affectualization. According to Volkan, the first manifestation of it

is usually an accumulation of memories and fantasies (flooding in the ideational field) that support the same emotion. The patient can refer to these memories or fantasies only in a kind of "shorthand" — fragmentary sentences, or a single word. He may then begin stuttering and lose the power of intelligible speech altogether. It is impossible at this point to distinguish between flooding in the emotional, actional, or ideational field. The patient may scream and exhibit diffuse motor activity; he may seem to have lost his human identity. . . . Patients capable of reporting their experience of emotional flooding after the event usually indicate that strange perceptual changes took place. They underwent a "metamorphosis" during the experience, becoming monstrous and diabolical when signal affects were replaced by primal affects closely related to the aggressive drive. [pp. 179, 183]

Such emotional outbursts are of little psychotherapeutic use. During them, the patient does not seem amenable to interpretive interventions; not enough observing ego is available to him. Their usefulness lies in their detoxifying effects over a long period of therapy and in their providing foci for proper, in-depth investigation during calmer times. While they are occurring, the therapist must avoid action in response. Although he must protect himself and the patient if that becomes necessary, in general he should stay unperturbed and attentive, almost to the point of appearing unaffected by the storm. This is integral to the holding environment and is silently reassuring to the patient; a parent's non-anxious, non-retaliatory resolve in face of a child's temper tantrum is a developmental counterpart to such "containment." Another intervention useful in such circumstances is simply to name the overwhelming emotion. Katan (1961) made this point when she said that "verbalization leads to an increase of the controlling function of the ego over affects and drives" (p. 185). Volkan also reports a patient who was helped by being addressed by her name during the emotional outburst; this gave her a handle for cognitive restabilization. Thus calmly "absorbing" the affective spill, naming the emotion, and gently providing small cognitive anchors are the methods by which the therapist can bring the emotional flooding under control.

SUGGESTED READINGS

Bibring, G. L., Dwyer, T. F., Huntington, D. S., and Valenstein, A. F. (1961). A study of the psychological processes in pregnancy and of the earliest mother–child relationship. *Psychoanalytic Study of the Child* 16:9–72. New York: International Universities Press.

Katan, A. (1961). Some thoughts about the role of verbalization in early childhood. *Psychoanalytic Study of the Child* 16:184–188. New York: International Universities Press.

Volkan, V. D. (1976). *Primitive Internalized Object Relations*, pp. 165–200. New York: International Universities Press.

76. How does the concept of *optimal distance* guide therapeutic intervention?

The concept of *optimal distance* was introduced into psychoanalytic literature by Maurice Bouvet in 1958 and later found greater exposition in the clinical psychoanalytic work of Michael Balint and the child developmental observations of Margaret Mahler. *A Janus-faced concept with both interpersonal and intrapsychic referents, optimal distance can be defined at two levels: preoedipal and oedipal.* At the preoedipal level, optimal distance is best viewed as a psychic position that permits intimacy without loss of autonomy, and separateness without painful aloneness. At the oedipal level, it can be viewed as the capacity to renounce primary oedipal objects in a way that (on the aggressive side) permits individual autonomy without sacrifice of traditional continuity and (on the libidinal side) establishment of the incest barrier without total obliteration of aim-inhibited, cross-generational eroticism.

Individuals with severe personality disorders lack the capacity to maintain optimal distance. The failure to achieve object constancy leads to a continued propensity to rely excessively on external objects for self-regulation. Aggression toward them mobilizes fears of having internally destroyed them, and this, in turn, fuels the need to monitor them closely in reality. Libidinal attachment and anaclitic longings, by contrast, stir up fears of enslavement by external objects, hence necessitating withdrawal from them. In the sexual and aggressive realms too, such individuals fear either overwhelming and being overwhelmed by others or being totally ineffectual and rejected by others. In light of this it is not surprising that the issue of optimal distance plays a significant role in their treatment.

Starting from the time the patient begins treatment, through interruptions, vacations, accidental extra-analytic encounters, transference-based oscillations of intimacy, termination-phase advances and regressions, and even afterward, the issue of optimal distance affects therapeutic technique (Akhtar 1992). The therapist has to be constantly mindful of the patient's need for closeness and autonomy and the two corresponding anxieties of fusion and abandonment. He must respect the patient's need to control the intrapsychic boundaries between conscious and unconscious processes, and between the self and the other. He must repeatedly demonstrate to the patient that he is aware of the latter's anxieties in this regard. This might require the therapist to state verbally that he knows that the patient wants him to remain optimally distant (and optimally close!). It might also require the therapist to avoid interpretive intrusions and knowingly restrict the expanse of his comments. The initial stirrings of longing in a previously detached schizoid patient or a violent enactment in an otherwise agreeable borderline patient, for instance, are better interpreted, at first, in the extratransference realm without too quickly unmasking their transference allusions. The optimal-distance concept also enriches the understanding of negative therapeutic reactions as these might also arise from separation-based concerns and fears of losing the analyst by getting better (besides being caused by unconscious oedipal guilt). Yet another way this concept guides technique is by increasing the therapist's sensitivity to the disorganizing effects of separation on the patient. The therapist might touch base with the patient by phone or with an extra appointment. Such availability provides auxiliary regulation pending enhanced self-regulation by the patient.

SUGGESTED READINGS

Akhtar, S. (1992). Tethers, orbits, and invisible fences: clinical, developmental, sociocultural, and technical aspects of optimal distance. In *When the Body Speaks: Psychological Meanings in Kinetic Clues*, ed. S. Kramer and S. Akhtar, pp. 21–57. Northvale, NJ: Jason Aronson.

Bouvet, M. (1958). Technical variation and the concept of distance. *International Journal of Psycho-Analysis* 39:211–221.

Escoll, P. (1992). Vicissitudes of optimal distance through the life cycle. In *When the Body Speaks: Psychological Meanings in Kinetic Clues*, ed. S. Kramer and S. Akhtar, pp. 59–87. Northvale, NJ: Jason Aronson.

77. What are *developmental interventions*?

In the treatment of severe character pathology, an extremely important ingredient is the establishment of a secure holding environment within which the psychotherapeutic process unfolds. This, in turn, is characterized by a dialectical relationship between the interpretive resolution of psychopathology and the resumption of arrested psychic growth. With each undoing of some aspect of pathology there is the opportunity for resumed development in that area, and with each such developmental advance there is an enhancement of the patient's tolerance for the exposure of unacceptable, anxiety-provoking wishes and fantasies.

It is in this context that Samuel Abrams's (1978) concept of *developmental intervention* offers itself as a specific technical tool. Abrams states that when a hitherto unexpressed healthy capacity emerges as a result of interpretive work, the analyst should underscore the progressive trend inherent in it. Calvin Settlage's (1993) recommendation that the analyst acknowledge and encourage the patient's developmental initiatives belongs in the same realm. Interventions of this sort can be made in both psychoanalysis and psychoanalytic psychotherapy.

How is this to be translated in terms of actual clinical interventions? In the majority of cases, the developmental intervention remains at the verbal level. Comments such as the following illustrate the use of this tool. "We can observe that you are now feeling capable of seeing things from someone else's point of view also." Or, "It is significant that you were able to experience yourself in a mixed light, not as the usual all-good or all-bad." Or, "It is interesting that you now wish to be regarded as special by me and, in view of the fact that you had never experienced this ordinary childhood feeling, its emergence is welcome in some ways."

In rare instances, actual action on the part of the therapist might be necessary to convey such developmental support. This is evident in the following vignette.

An extremely ascetic, depressed, and socially isolated woman with a childhood of profound neglect and abuse, made a request of me after three years of psychotherapy. I had moved into a new office and the changed seating arrangement forced her to face a certain painting that she said she did not like. She requested that I put it elsewhere in the office. While curious about the potential meaning of the request, I sensed something different at work here. The patient had begun experiencing entitlement! I therefore responded by saying, "It is encouraging that you can allow yourself to demand something of me. Now, as it happens I rather like the painting and its location so I would not remove it altogether. However, in keeping with your desire, I will take it off the wall before each of your sessions so that you will not have to look at it." I reliably did so for about three or four months, after which she said that it was fine with her if I stopped the practice. (Deeper understanding of the meanings of this request came much later.)

Developmental interventions provide the patient a greater access to the silent progressive trends activated by the treatment.

Such access would be valuable on several accounts. For one thing, it is worthwhile to have a conscious awareness of any area of unconscious activity; for another, aiding in the distinction between the progressive and regressive may result in a further sharpening of the expressions of the transference neurosis; and lastly, by rendering a progressive potential into consciousness, one might facilitate the emergence of experiential building-blocks necessary for development [Abrams 1978, p. 397]

SUGGESTED READINGS

Abrams, S. (1978). The teaching and learning of psychoanalytic developmental psychology. *Journal of the American Psychoanalytic Association* 26:387–406.

Kramer, S. (1987). A contribution to the concept "The Exception" as a developmental phenomenon. *Child Abuse and Neglect* 11:367–370.

Settlage, C. (1993). Therapeutic process and developmental process in the restructuring of object and self constancy. *Journal of the American Psychoanalytic Association* 41:473–492.

78. What underlies the frequent and painful disruptions of the therapeutic alliance and how should one manage such crises?

A puzzling phenomenon that occurs quite frequently in the treatment of individuals with severe character pathology is the repeated rupture of the working alliance between the patient and the therapist. A relatively harmonious working compact between the two suddenly turns into an adversarial relationship. The patient begins to feel misunderstood and experiences the therapist as unempathic. "You just don't understand me," the patient repeats plaintively and monotonously. Efforts on the therapist's part to help translate the patient's agony into words fail miserably. More misunderstanding develops. Nothing seems to be working. It is as if the two parties had suddenly begun speaking two different languages.

Such disruptions of the therapeutic alliance have been discussed in depth by Michael Balint, Heinz Kohut, and his followers, especially Ernst Wolf. These authors have also outlined technical maneuvers to handle such difficult moments in therapy. According to them, crises of this sort happen when the therapist "fails to 'click-in,' that is, to respond as the patient expects him to" (Balint 1968, p. 19) or when the patient is "suffering a disappointment in the idealized analyst" (Kohut 1971, p. 98) or when there develops a "discrepancy between the experiences of reality" (Wolf 1994, p. 94) by the two parties. While differing in terminology, the three theorists are essentially proposing the same mechanism: *a painful disruption happens when the smoothness of the fit between the patient and the therapist is brought to a halt by a malattunement of the therapist toward the patient's psychic reality*. Consequently, the three authors suggest similar *technical interventions*. In their view, the therapist should acknowledge that he has been experienced as malattuned. In doing so "(1) he provides the patient with an experience of having effectively communicated to the analyst, that is, a self-enhancing experience of efficacy, and (2) he restores the patient's experience of a selfobject bond with the analyst" (Wolf 1994, p. 94). Therapists' acknowledgment of malattunement paves the way for a collaborative inquiry into the dynamic and genetic causes of the disruption.

While such affirmative and stabilizing interventions are undeniably useful, I suspect that there is much more to such disruptions and therefore other interventions should also be kept in mind. *Other factors that might precipitate such disruptions* include (1) the mobilization of the *patient's hatred* toward the therapist who, after all, stands not only for the hoped-for, idealized parent but also for the "unempathic," hated parent; (2) *a fear of abandonment by the therapist* if things keep going well for too long; (3) *defensive retreat* from oedipal level conflicts (which the patient only dimly understands) to the anguished but more familiar "deprived baby" stance, and (4) finally, *negative therapeutic reactions* based on guilt from a variety of real and imaginary causes that represent various levels of development.

In light of the possibility that many factors (alone or in combination) can trigger painful disruptions of the therapeutic alliance, a one-track approach to its understanding and management cannot be recommended. Acknowledgment of the therapist's malattunement and affirmation of the patient's distress must lead not only to a search for similar childhood experiences but also to an investigation of the potentially defensive uses of a familiar form of distress.

SUGGESTED READINGS

Balint, M. (1968). *The Basic Fault*. New York: Brunner/Mazel.

Kohut, H. (1971). *The Analysis of the Self*, pp. 74–101. New York: International Universities Press.

Wolf, E. (1994). Selfobject experiences: development, psychopathology, treatment. In *Mahler and Kohut: Perspectives on Development, Psychopathology, and Technique*, ed. S. Kramer and S. Akhtar, pp. 65–96. Northvale, NJ: Jason Aronson.

79. What motives underlie a patient's suicidal preoccupation?

In 1938, Karl Menninger outlined three paradigmatic constellations of suicidal intent: those pertaining to hopelessness, impotent rage, and guilt. Respectively, these fundamental motifs are represented in the wish to die, the (inverted) wish to kill, and the wish to be killed.

(1) *The wish to die*: Hopelessness leading to a wish to die is seen most often in schizoid personalities or in other severe personality disorders undergoing a schizoid regression. These phenomena have been most meaningfully addressed by the independent group of British analysts. This group sees the individual with a basic deficit in his psychostructural organizations involved in a lifelong quest. This quest is for a relationship that will provide optimal conditions for a safe regression, containment of aggression, shedding of lifelong pretenses, and regrowth of the core personality. The therapeutic relationship should, and usually does, offer such a possibility and therefore enhances the patient's hope. Empathic failures of the therapist and ruptures of the continuity of the therapeutic hours dash the patient's hopes and precipitate a painful sense of futility. Life appears worthless, and the theme of suicide enters the scene.

(2) *The (inverted) wish to kill*: The second paradigmatic constellation involves impotent rage and the inverted wish to kill oneself "coupled with a fantasy that one's death will make the significant object either recognize one's worth or be crushed by guilt feelings" (Kernberg et al. 1990, p. 154). This constellation is seen most often in borderline and histrionic individuals. Transferences related to the wish for revenge seem the prime motivator of such behavior. Suicidal threats and gestures become ways to coercively dominate or manipulate the environment.

(3) *The wish to be killed*: This is the dynamic constellation seen in depressive neurotics as well as in the later phases of the

treatment of narcissistic characters. Their wish to be killed (punished) stems from guilt. This guilt, though involving oedipal issues, is largely based on the patient's becoming (after months or years of psychotherapeutic work) aware of his aggression toward the therapist and developing genuine concern for him. Now the patient might "feel despair because he has mistreated the analyst and all the significant persons in his life, and he may feel that he has actually destroyed those whom he could have loved and who might have loved him. Now he may have intense suicidal thoughts and intentions" (Kernberg 1975, p. 258).

It is worth considering whether the three dynamic constellations could be responded to by matching psychotherapeutic strategies. For instance, the hopelessness dynamic may be met with "affirmative interventions" (Killingmo 1989), the impotent rage dynamic with limit setting and interpretive interventions, and the guilt dynamic with a mixture of facilitation of mourning and interpretive interventions. However, this line of thinking tends to oversimplify things, since in clinical practice the three constellations neither exhaust the list of motivations underlying suicidal intent nor occur in pure form. The greater advantage of knowing them is that such knowledge might enhance the therapist's ability to empathize with the patient, understand him, and thus become able to make better attuned interventions.

SUGGESTED READINGS

Kernberg, O. F. (1975). *Borderline Conditions and Pathological Narcissism*. New York: Jason Aronson.

Kernberg, O. F., Selzer, M. A., Koenigsberg, H. W., et al. (1990). *Psychodynamic Psychotherapy of Borderline Patients*. New York: Basic Books.

Menninger, K. A. (1938). *Man against Himself*. New York: Harcourt.

80. Under what circumstances does the patient's talk of suicide necessitate active interventions?

Individuals with severe personality disorders often express wishes to die and even talk of committing suicide. Most of the time such communications can be handled within the traditional affirmative-interpretive modes of psychoanalytic work. There are, however, two situations in which a more active intervention on the therapist's part might become necessary.

First and foremost is the acute situation of a patient's beginning to talk seriously of committing suicide. This poses a technical challenge for the therapist, who is faced with the difficult task of assessing the actual risk to the patient's life. Switching from a receptive-contemplative mode to a more directly interrogative mode might now become inevitable. The therapist must gauge the intensity of the patient's suicidal ideation, the existence and clarity of plans, the availability of means, the depth of depression, the extent of social isolation, the amount of alcohol and drug intake, and the degree to which the patient's communications are trustworthy. If there are definite plans, available means, insufficient social support, heavy drinking and drug abuse, severe depression, including the ominous feeling of having no alternative, and if there is doubt regarding the patient's reliability, then the therapist must act decisively. The course open to the therapist under such circumstances includes putting the patient on antidepressant medication, informing relatives, assuring the removal of the means for intended suicide, and hospitalizing the patient, which may, at times, have to be against the patient's wishes. Whether such radical departures from neutrality threaten the future possibility of the patient's continuing in psychoanalytic psychotherapy with the same therapist is something that can await assessment at a later time. At the moment of a serious suicidal risk, however, protecting the patient is the prime consideration.

A second manner in which the theme of suicide enters the

treatment is by self-destructive threats becoming incorporated into the patient's way of life. Kernberg and colleagues (1990) emphatically suggest that faced with such a situation

> the therapist should tell the family that the patient is chronically apt to commit suicide, indicating to them that the patient suffers from a psychological illness with a definite risk of mortality. The therapist should express to those concerned the willingness to engage in a therapeutic effort to help the patient overcome the illness, but should neither give firm assurance of success nor guarantee protection from suicide over the long period of treatment. This realistic circumscription of the treatment may be the most effective way to protect the therapeutic relationship from the destructive involvements of family members and from the patient's efforts to control the therapy by inducing in the therapist a countertransference characterized by guilt feelings and paranoid fears regarding third parties. [pp. 156–157]

In addition to the two situations mentioned above, the phase of developing an initial contract might also involve more direct, limit-setting types of interventions vis-à-vis the patient's suicidal impulses. This is especially true while dealing with individuals with borderline personality disorders. The main purpose of these interventions is to safeguard the therapist's technical neutrality and protect the intrapsychic exploratory work from the behavioral attacks of the patient.

SUGGESTED READINGS

Kernberg, O. F. (1984). *Severe Personality Disorders: Psychotherapeutic Strategies*, pp. 254–263. New Haven, CT: Yale University Press.

Kernberg, O. F., Selzer, M. A., Koenigsberg, H. W., et al. (1990). *Psychodynamic Psychotherapy of Borderline Patients*. New York: Basic Books.

Yeomans, E., Selzer, M. A., and Clarkin, J. F. (1992). *Treating the Borderline Patient: A Contract Based Approach*. New York: Basic Books.

81. What are some basic guidelines for hospital management of borderline patients?

First and foremost, the purpose of hospitalization should be squarely kept in mind. Short-term hospitalization for borderline patients is indicated largely for crisis management, diagnostic, and triage purposes. Long term hospitalization is indicated for

> patients whose personality characteristics militate against outpatient therapy but who can benefit from dynamic therapy in a setting that enables them to tolerate it. These are patients with minimal motivation for change, minimal capacity for reasonable cooperation with the treatment, uncontrollable generalized impulsivity, minimal introspection in spite of normal intelligence, and a cultural and premorbid background that would ordinarily signal a capacity for symbolic thinking and communication. [Kernberg et al. 1989, p. 179]

Remembering the aims of hospitalization prevents unrealistic expectations of the staff from both themselves and the patient.

Second, the staff must strive toward a therapeutic attitude that consists of four aspects: (1) an acceptance of the fact that one will inevitably be the recipient of the patient's rage and provocativeness, (2) a regard for the view that all behavior has multiple determinants; this will prevent either/or types of arguments regarding the meanings of the patient's verbal or nonverbal communications; (3) an unshakeable determination to maintain communication with each other with no secret transactions with the patient (except, of course, the individual therapist's protecting the confidentiality of the information gathered during the therapy hours); and (4) an acknowledgment by the staff (and the unit as a whole) of its not being omnipotent and occasionally requiring "extramural" input (e.g., consultation from an attending therapist on another unit) when faced with problematic situations.

Third, the hospital unit must provide a secure holding environment with a consistent and comfortable physical setting and a psychological atmosphere of non-retaliation, curiosity, and lack of judgment. The patient's needs must be viewed as more important than the staff's needs so that the patient does not become "used" in the staff struggles or is unempathically reduced to a generic problem.

Fourth, the hospital unit must view itself as a structure which, to a greater or lesser extent, is expected to be internalized by the patient. (Clearly, the longer the hospitalization, the more this applies.) Therefore, the unit must be able to (1) institute limit setting without a punitive agenda, (2) promote delay of action by interposing the requirement of thinking about impulses (e.g., a patient's requests of almost any sort should receive the message: "Let us think about it"), (3) respect the patient's autonomy yet maintain connectedness, (4) teach the patient to solve complex tasks by breaking them down into smaller segments, and (5) support, reinforce, and reward the patient's positive behaviors. In connection with the last mentioned, it is important that the patient's own talents (painting, mechanical repair, ledger keeping, etc.) be enlisted in any activities program designed to make him feel productive and contributory to the unit.

Finally, the administrative structure of the unit should allow for (1) clear designation of authority regarding various aspects of patient care, (2) group interventions with patients on the unit and, separately, with staff members as well, and (3) availability for solid social work support for planning outpatient care following discharge.

SUGGESTED READINGS

Kernberg, O. F. (1984). *Severe Personality Disorders: Psychotherapeutic Strategies*, pp. 27–51. New Haven, CT: Yale University Press.

Kernberg, O. F., Selzer, M. A., Koenigsberg, H. W., et al. (1989). *Psychodynamic Psychotherapy of Borderline Patients*. New York: Basic Books.

Schulz, C. G. (1987). The struggle toward ambivalence. In *Attachment and the Therapeutic Process*, J. L. Sacksteder, D. P. Schwartz, and Y. Akabane pp. 223–238. Madison, CT: International Universities Press.

82. Is there any role of self-disclosure on the therapist's part in the treatment of borderline individuals?

It is clearly inappropriate and antitherapeutic for a therapist to discuss his own traumatic experiences, sexuality, marital life, legal and financial concerns, religious views, and so forth with a patient. However, the ground becomes shaky when it comes to less "stimulating" matters, especially during extraordinary circumstances and with patients who have the capacity to mobilize powerful rescue fantasies in the countertransference.

The issue, therefore, is more complex than whether to disclose or not. It involves other questions—What to disclose? How much to disclose? When? To whom? To what end? And, finally, how to determine whether one's decision has been appropriate. It is in the setting of such complexity that I suggest that there are three forms of self-disclosure: integral, situational, and technical.

(1) *Integral*: Some self-disclosure is inevitable in just our being with the patient. Our names and skin color betray our ethnic and racial identities. Our office decor reveals our cultural dimension. Such inevitable self-disclosures are, of course, more marked for patients who themselves are in the mental health field. While all this can undergo transference elaborations, it is naïve to maintain a belief in our total opacity. (2) *Situational*: This involves the therapist's departing from his usual anonymity because it seems essential either for protecting the therapeutic framework and/or for shielding the patient's ego from severe pain and regressive deformation. For instance, when the therapist suddenly has to take a considerable time off (e.g., for major surgery) or when he is under severe strain (e.g., illness, mourning), he might need to give some actual information to the patient. However, the degree and timing of such disclosure have to be tailored to each specific patient's life history and ego assets. Consultation with a

supervisor or a trusted colleague is helpful in such circumstances. (3) *Technical*: As a carefully chosen strategy, limited self disclosure can be useful. Bollas (1992), for instance, describes the analyst's occasionally sharing his own free associations with the patient: "You know, as you are speaking I have a picture of a little girl of three. . . ." (p. 121), and so on. Bollas discusses the risks of such an intervention and provides guidelines for its use. I have often found myself disclosing a snippet of my association right *after* the patient has arrived at a certain understanding that to me seems correct. For example, I might say, "You know, just when you connected this guilty feeling to your mother, I, too, was thinking about your relationship with her, especially when. . . ." and so on. Roger Lewin (Lewin and Schulz 1992) has taken such "role sanctioned self-disclosure" a step further by including information from his childhood in such exchanges with the patient. To me this appears excessive, as it might burden the patient.

The decision to make a self-disclosure is correct if it is followed by the patient's feeling peaceful and able to cooperate better with the treatment (though not without transference elaborations of the information received). The disclosure is "incorrect" (in nature, timing, or dosage) if it results in further demands, ego regression, or profoundly guilty reactions on the patient's part. Unfortunately, one can determine this only in retrospect. The decision is always risky and the novice would do better to err on the side of caution.

SUGGESTED READINGS

Bollas, C. (1992). *Being a Character: Psychoanalysis and Self Experience*, pp. 101–133. New York: Hill and Wang.

Lewin, R., and Schulz, C. (1992). *Losing and Fusing: Borderline Transitional Object and Self Relations*, pp. 301–322. Northvale, NJ: Jason Aronson.

Searles, H. F. (1979). *Countertransference and Related Subjects: Selected Papers*, pp. 380–460. New York: International Universities Press.

83. What are the sources, manifestations, and risks of countertransference hatred?

Individuals with severe personality disorders, especially those with borderline features, tend to develop intense negative transferences. However, they also "love" and need the therapist and therefore feel guilty about their hatred of him. As a result, they project it onto the therapist, insisting that *he* hates *them*. This justifies their own assaults on the therapist. These attacks can be in the form of sarcastic remarks, angry silences, frequent schedule changes, and, at times, grossly destructive actions aimed at the therapist's person or property. Ultimately, the therapist does begin to feel hatred towards the patient. This countertransference experience contains elements of both aversion and malice, though one of these aspects might be more conscious than the other. Aversion leads to the wish to withdraw from the patient and abandon him. Malice leads to cruel impulses toward the patient manifesting as sarcasm, inflexibility, and more direct hurtful actions.

Fortunately, most therapists realize that it is antitherapeutic to live out their countertransference aversion and malice in relation to a patient. Viewing themselves as compassionate and caring individuals, therapists are prone to unconsciously mobilize defenses against such countertransference hatred. These are intended to protect the therapist from a fuller and deeper awareness of his hatred of the patient. John Maltsberger and Dan Buie (1974) have outlined five such defensive postures:

(1) *Repression*: This might give rise to lack of interest in working with the patient, chronic boredom, excessive daydreaming during the sessions, frequent and obvious looking at the clock, and, worse still, forgetting the patient's appointments.

(2) *Turning against the self*: The therapist using this defense becomes doubtful about his therapeutic skills, excessively self-critical, and masochistically submissive to the patient. This last

mentioned tendency is more marked in those therapists who are characterologically prone to guilt and self-punishment.

(3) *Reaction formation*: The therapist using reaction formation might become excessively helpful ("pitiless hospitality" in Salman Rushdie's terms!) with omnipotent rescue fantasies and unrealistic interventions in the patient's real life. The defensive nature of such "therapeutic zeal" is betrayed not only by their anxious rigidity but often by their results as well.

(4) *Projection*: Here the therapist begins to dread that the patient will commit suicide. "This kind of preoccupation is usually accompanied by some degree of fear (the consequence of projected malice), and with a degree of aversion, i.e., the patient seems abominable" (Maltsberger and Buie 1974, p. 629).

(5) *Distortion and denial of reality for validation of counter-transference hatred*: In order to rationalize his hatred, the therapist might distort clinical facts and ignore important information. As a result, he might transfer, prematurely discharge, or altogether abandon the patient.

Since countertransference hatred is truly risky when it is kept out of awareness, it becomes very important to recognize the above-mentioned defensive postures. Only when such countertransference can be brought and kept into awareness can it give rise to useful interventions.

SUGGESTED READINGS

Maltsberger, J. T., and Buie, D. H. (1974). Countertransference hate in the treatment of suicidal patients. *Archives of General Psychiatry* 30:625–633.

Searles, H. F. (1967). The "dedicated physician" in psychotherapy and psychoanalysis. In *Crosscurrents in Psychiatry and Psychoanalysis*, ed. R. W. Gibson, pp. 128–146. Philadelphia: J. B. Lippincott.

Winnicott, D. W. (1949). Hate in the countertransference. *International Journal of Psycho-Analysis* 30:69–74.

84. What are the technical strategies vis-à-vis intense hatred in the transference-countertransference axis?

The technical strategies vis-à-vis intense hatred in the treatment situation can be divided into the following categories.

(1) *Containment*: The therapeutic situation must be such that it can "absorb" the patient's hatred. The non-judgmental and non-retaliatory stance of the therapist, whose concern and commitment to the patient survive despite the latter's assaults, goes a long way to accomplish this goal. The therapist's ability to maintain firm limits and to protect the patient as well as himself from harm also contribute to the patient's feeling that his hatred can be "tamed" (i.e., brought under the control of his ego).

(2) *Affirmative interventions:* The therapist must be able to demonstrate to the patient his understanding of the latter's predicament. He should make interventions that accept, objectify, and justify the patient's affective experience. The patient must come to see that the therapist regards his hatred as understandable and valid, given his psychic experience of past and current reality. He might make statements like, "I can see that you feel nothing but hatred toward me and, given your experience of the situation right now, this seems quite a legitimate response to me." It is only after such affirmation that the patient can be engaged in an inquiry into the hidden sources and meanings of his hatred. This movement from affirmation to interpretation can sometimes be accomplished in the same session. At other times, one has to wait longer.

(3) *Interpretive interventions*: The therapist must interpret the deeper aspects of the patient's hatred. These involve the transference distortion of the therapist as a cold and uncaring person. Sources of such a belief lie in the patient's actual experience of uncaring parents, hostile exaggeration of the parental failures, or attribution to the therapist of the patient's own scorn and hatred

of him. However, in thinking along these lines it should not be overlooked that the patient's hatred can also serve defensive purposes against more frightening feelings of dependence and love toward the therapist.

(4) *"Spoiling" of the pleasure in hatred*: The therapist also needs to help the patient become aware of the sadistic pleasure inherent in his hatred. Making this conscious, by interpreting defenses against such awareness, weakens the patient's victim-like stance. This renders his hatred somewhat ego-dystonic, hence more amenable to interpretive resolution.

(5) *Finally, there is the difficult matter of the therapist's justified hate of the patient.* Winnicott (1947) not only talks of such rational hatred on the part of the therapist, but also of the technical implications of such conceptualization. He proposes that "in certain stages of certain analyses the analyst's hate is actually sought by the patient, and what is then needed is hate that is objective. If the patient seeks objective or justified hate he must be able to reach it, else he cannot feel he can reach objective love" (p. 199). Winnicott goes on to raise the matter of disclosure of the analyst's hate to the patient:

> This is obviously a matter fraught with danger, and it needs the most careful timing. But I believe an analysis is incomplete if even towards the end it has not been possible for the analyst to tell the patient what he, the analyst, did unbeknown for the patient whilst he was ill, in the early stages. Until this interpretation is made the patient is kept to some extent in the position of infant—one who can not understand what he owes to his mother. [p. 202]

SUGGESTED READINGS

Akhtar, S., Kramer, S., and Parens, H., eds. (1995). *The Birth of Hatred: Clinical, Developmental, and Technical Aspects of Intense Aggression.* Northvale, NJ: Jason Aronson.

Kernberg, O. F. (1992). *Aggression in Personality Disorders and Perversions*, pp. 21–32. New Haven, CT: Yale University Press.

Winnicott, D. W. (1947). Hate in the countertransference. In *Through Paediatrics to Psychoanalysis: Collected Papers*, pp. 194–203, Brunner/Mazel: New York, 1992.

85. How can the therapist manage difficult countertransference feelings?

Intense countertransference feelings are frequent during in-depth psychotherapy of borderline, narcissistic, and schizoid patients. On the one hand, their tendency toward idealization and their traumatized and poignant lives stir up rescue fantasies in the therapist. On the other hand, their ruthless devaluation of the help offered, their sadistic provocations (through verbal barbs or actions such as lateness, withholding payments, frequent or anonymous phone calls, etc.), and their assaults upon the therapist's self-esteem, mobilize hatred in the latter. At first, these feelings are mild and fleeting. As the treatment proceeds, however, they become deeper and more sustained. While such countertransference can be quite informative, it can also pose a hazard for the therapeutic process. The risk is greater if it remains unrecognized by the therapist. The novice especially needs to be aware of the following guidelines regarding the management of countertransference.

(1) *Self care*: First and foremost, the therapist himself must receive enough libidinal supplies and ego support. Of course, a basically "good" internal world with a well-developed sublimatory capacity goes a long way in this regard. From outside, however, this can be assured by having a loving mate or an empathic friend with some sense of humor, a limited proportion of severely ill patients in one's case load, and the ego freedom to occasionally take leave of one's therapeutic work and identity (e.g., during vacations).

(2) *Self education*: Reading the literature on countertransference is necessary for the therapist. It will expand his intellectual horizons and render his distressing experience less private. Similar help can be obtained by seeking supervision on a sustained basis while treating difficult patients. "Emergency" consultations with senior colleagues during crises can avert countertransference

enactments. The therapist's firm belief in "the principle of multiple function" (Waelder 1936) will also help in reducing his vulnerability to either/or conceptualizations regarding drive and defense, deficit and conflict, oedipal and preoedipal, and, most important, regarding his own love or hate.

(3) *Self scrutiny*: The therapist must remain highly vigilant about his affective tone both during and between the sessions with such patients. He must frequently examine his emotional state at the end of the day and scan for significant affective peaks and valleys. He must also ask himself questions such as, "How do I feel about this patient?" or "How did I really feel in that particular session?" on a frequent basis.

(4) *Self analysis*: Upon becoming aware of his strong feelings, the therapist (having undergone psychoanalysis or psychoanalytic psychotherapy himself) should seek to understand their origins. How much of this emotion is related to his own background? What proportion of it is strictly related to the therapeutic situation? Even in that situation, to what degree is the emotion a reflection of the patient's projective identification and to what degree is it a "rational" response on the part of the therapist? What is the patient trying to actualize by inducing such affects in the therapist? In experiencing such affects who is it that the therapist is becoming? These sorts of questions might assist the therapist facing difficult countertransference situations to get in touch with his deeper motivations. This, in turn, will free his ego to select optimal and realistic therapeutic interventions.

SUGGESTED READINGS

Racker, H. (1957). The meanings and uses of countertransference. *Psychoanalytic Quarterly* 26:303–357.

Searles, H. F. (1979). The countertransference in psychoanalytic therapy with borderline patients. In *Advances in Psychotherapy of the Borderline Patient*, ed. J. LeBoit and A. Capponi, pp. 309–346. New York: Jason Aronson.

Waelder, R. (1936). The principle of multiple function. *Psychoanalytic Quarterly* 5:45–62.

86. Are there elements resembling mourning in the treatment of individuals with severe personality disorders?

Mourning-like elements are integral to all in-depth psychotherapies and analyses. In order to be modified, the patient's sexual and aggressive impulses must renounce their original aims, change objects, and find newer expressions. This is felt as a loss, which is compensated by burgeoning dominance of the ego over the unruly underground of infantile wishes and fears. The termination phase especially mobilizes mourning, not only because it involves actual separation from the therapist but also because of the loss of hope that treatment will solve all problems. One has to give up the expectations of omnipotence from both oneself and one's therapist.

While this applies to all patients, it is true that *mourning-like elements carry much greater significance in the treatment of individuals with severe character pathology*. This is in part because they have often suffered severe, actual traumas in their childhoods. More important, they have not gone through the incremental steps of loss (of external support, of omnipotence) and gain (of internal structure, of reality principle) typical of the separation-individuation process. Lacking this prototype of mourning, they suffer from two predicaments. On the one hand, they cannot go over losses without serious setbacks. On the other hand, they possess a "pathological hope" (Amati-Mehler and Argentieri 1989, p. 300) that an omnipotent rescuer will come and solve all their problems.

Psychotherapeutic or psychoanalytic work with such patients must attend to these issues. First, their actual childhood losses and traumas must be respected and empathized with (without overlooking the "screen" nature of such memories). Second, the degree to which they can hold on to an inner image of the therapist during weekends and vacations should be unobtrusively assessed. In cases where there is a clear propensity toward losing the internalized image of the analyst (with associated panic, emptiness, and disorientation), the therapist might decide to touch base with the patient by telephone or through an extra appointment. (The effects of such departures from the ordinary framework should be looked for and analyzed later on.) Such availability provides auxiliary regulation while the patient's self-regulatory capacity is still developing. Third, later in the treatment the therapist might need to address the patient's other difficulty with mourning, that is, his or her pathological optimism. The therapist needs to make this blind optimism conscious and interpret its narcissistic and masochistic aspects (since excessive hope about the future keeps the patient suffering in the present). The therapist might even need to rupture the patient's pathological hope, though very tactfully and never without demonstrating to the latter that the potential for moving from excessive to realistic hope is inherent in him. Finally, the therapist must facilitate the mourning process mobilized by termination. He should be prepared for a longer than usual termination phase and should enable the patient to appreciate his own contributions to the treatment in order to reduce the omnipotent view of the therapist. On the other hand, he must also help the patient accept the remnant psychic vulnerability as a realistic limit of what treatment can achieve. The therapist should not taper the frequency of sessions and create the illusion that mourning can be bypassed. Indeed, the patient might even be told that this mourning will continue after the treatment has ended, though he will be able to manage it on his own.

SUGGESTED READINGS

Amati-Mehler, J., and Argentieri, S. (1989). Hope and hopelessness: a technical problem? *International Journal of Psycho-Analysis* 70:295–304.

Balint, M. (1968). *The Basic Fault: Therapeutic Aspects of Regression*, pp. 183–184. London: Tavistock.

Kernberg, O. F., Selzer, M. A., Koenigsberg, H. W., et al. (1989). *Psychodynamic Psychotherapy of Borderline Patients*, pp. 137–143, 149–150. New York: Basic Books.

87. What is *negative therapeutic reaction* and how should it be handled?

The term *negative therapeutic reaction* was coined by Freud in 1923. He used it to denote the paradoxical worsening of some patients after a seemingly successful and productive piece of therapeutic work is accomplished. In some instances, even a single correct interpretation has this paradoxical effect. Referring to such patients, Freud (1923) stated, " . . . every partial solution that ought to result, and in other people does result, in an improvement or a temporary suspension of symptoms produces in them for the time being an exacerbation of their illness" (p. 49). There are many possible causes for negative therapeutic reaction, with the following four being most prominent among them:

(1) *Unconscious guilt*: A common cause of negative therapeutic reaction is unconscious guilt. This derives from childhood fantasies of having committed a "crime" and therefore deserving, even needing, punishment. The nature of such imaginary crimes varies greatly. A frequent theme involves the dual oedipal transgressions of incest and murder. The resulting need for suffering is gratified by the masochistic aspects of psychopathology and, when that is threatened by successful therapeutic intervention, by a negative therapeutic reaction.

(2) *Problematic identifications*: Another determinant of negative therapeutic reaction is an ego ideal constituted largely of identifications with a masochistic parent who idealized a life of suffering. Such integration of self-destructiveness into the ego ideal leads the patient to undermine every therapeutic advance; becoming healthy, under such circumstances, is tantamount to betraying the suffering parent. This constellation often heralds an unfavorable outcome.

(3) *Separation-related issues*: Even more pernicious negative therapeutic reactions are based on unresolved preoedipal issues including (a) a feeling of guilt in having an autonomous and

separate existence from the mother, and (b) a characterological defense against the dread of symbiotic fusion with her. A narcissistically needy mother who cannot let go of her child renders him vulnerable to unconsciously equating separation with causing injury to her, even killing her. Asch (1976) notes that certain "specific accusations by mother (your birth was so difficult, I almost died; I was so torn up inside) often add fixating elements of historical 'reality'" (p. 392) to such fears. Subsequent separations from primary objects (and later, from their transferential recreations) provoke anxiety and are dreaded. With each progressive movement in their treatment, such patients develop a fear of abandonment by the therapist and therefore regressively lose the newly acquired insights.

(4) *Envy*: Yet another cause of negative therapeutic reaction is the patient's deep envy of the therapist's ability to soothe him, to give him something useful to ponder in the form of interpretation. That the therapist does not appear to be as unfortunate as the patient, seems free of psychic turmoil, and appears to possess patience and creativity, lead the patient to feel hateful envy of him. This, in turn, propels the patient to undo the benefit received from the therapist's interpretation.

Keeping these four factors in mind and remembering that more than one dynamic might be active at a time should help the psychotherapist formulate useful interventions.

SUGGESTED READINGS

Asch, S. (1976). Varieties of negative therapeutic reaction and problems of technique. *Journal of the American Psychoanalytic Association* 24:383–407.

Freud, S. (1923). The ego and the id. *Standard Edition* 19:1–66.

Sandler, J., Dare, C., and Holder, A. (1973). The negative therapeutic reaction. In *The Patient and the Analyst*, pp. 84–93. New York: International Universities Press.

88. What does the increasing predominance of oedipal transferences imply about the course of treatment?

With the progress of treatment, the patient's splitting defense is increasingly replaced by repression, with the resulting salutory effect on self- and object constancy. Oedipal transferences now begin to occupy center stage with greater clarity and persistence. This occurrence is of crucial importance to the overall course of treatment and can result in two outcomes.

The first outcome is seen in patients who were very ego-impaired and whose treatments were characterized by profound sadomasochistic enactments, resulting in the therapist's frequent departure from neutrality. Such patients might end the treatment at this point. Their treatment appears to them as having reached a point of diminishing returns. They feel the exhilaration in their burgeoning ego capacities to be sufficient reward to consider termination. Paradoxically, psychic growth here takes the patients away from introspection. The need to exercise some of the newly acquired capacities in the external world becomes predominant. Another reason for such patients' wanting termination at this point is their inability to sustain the more subtle transferences of the oedipal phase in connection with the same therapist with whom they have charted the bloody seas of preoedipal issues. Many such patients return for work on oedipal issues, though often with a different therapist.

A second outcome is witnessed in less impaired patients. Here, after the mending of splitting of self- and object representations and the achievement of object constancy, oedipal transferences can be handled in the customary interpretive fashion. However, even these cases may present special difficulties. The oedipal transferences may continue to have a "narcissistic tinge" (Volkan 1987) that may need only a gentle recognition or a proper interpretive handling if it is marked. More important, there may be a continued tendency toward regressive reification of preoedipal structures. The deprived, hungry baby and the ruthless avenger self-images tend to be activated repeatedly, but now their transference aim is mainly one of a regressive defense against the more subtle, oedipal issues with less familiar, incestuous anxieties. A related development is the tendency toward a negative therapeutic reaction based on the fear that mastery of preoedipal issues might lead to a premature abandonment by the therapist (Grunert 1979). As a result, there might follow a transitional phase during which there is much back-and-forth activity between preoedipal and oedipal transferences. This is especially true, in my experience, for women who felt traumatically "dropped" by their mothers around age 2 or so and whose mothers also appeared to be unduly powerful oedipal rivals. Increasing psychosocial autonomy during treatment frightens them with premature loss of the therapist. Pleasure in newly acquired skills also becomes quickly associated with oedipal, hence guilt-ridden, ambitions. Together, such dynamic forces lead to frequent, often tenacious, regressions into a victimized babylike posture. Empathic comments conveying the therapist's awareness of these anxieties diminish the patients' aloneness with such fears. This, in turn, renders them amenable to interpretive resolution. Killingmo's (1989) recommendation of "oscillations in technique" (p. 77) between affirmation and interpretation is highly pertinent in this context. As the oedipal component of these issues is analyzed, termination becomes a real possibility.

SUGGESTED READINGS

Grunert, U. (1979). The negative therapeutic reaction as a reactivation of a disturbed process of the separation in the transference. *Bulletin of the European Psychoanalytic Federation* 16:5–19.

Killingmo, B. (1989). Conflict and deficit: implications for technique. *International Journal of Psycho-Analysis* 70:65–79.

Volkan, V. D. (1987). *Six Steps in the Treatment of Borderline Personality Organization*. Northvale, NJ: Jason Aronson.

89. How does one know that the treatment is coming to an end?

The end of the psychotherapeutic process is in sight with the occurrence of *certain structural achievements* including (1) a newly developed or enhanced capacity for experiencing and tolerating ambivalence; (2) a greater ability to empathize with others and the resultant deepening of object relations; (3) the emergence of a more realistic view of oneself; (4) a working through and renunciation of infantile omnipotence; (5) a strengthening of ego as evidenced by better impulse control, greater anxiety tolerance, and enhanced sublimatory tendencies; (6) a diminution of reliance on magical acts or fantasies and alcohol or drugs to control anxiety; (7) a greater capacity for peaceful aloneness; and (8) the gradual replacement of intense, predominantly preoedipal, transferences by relatively subtle oedipal transferences. These developments, however, only herald the beginning of the end, not the end itself. The increasing evidence of these capacities, both within the patient–therapist dyad and in the patient's outside life, constitutes the first flickering of the proverbial light at the end of the tunnel.

This process has emotional and cognitive reverberations in both parties. From the patient's perspective, there is (1) a greater trust in the therapist; (2) a true fondness for him — still based on idealization but now including an awareness of the therapist's occasional failures and his more sustained quirks and limitations; (3) a marked diminution or removal of presenting symptoms; (4) a deeper capacity for understanding his own self, resulting from an identification with the analyzing functions of the therapist; this is akin to what Peter Giovacchini (1972) has called the formation of an "analytic introject"; (5) a diminution in the felt need of the therapist, at times accompanied by anxiety and regressive clinging to the therapist; (6) a richer view of the parents and a changed relationship with them; and (7) a pleasurable increase in the range of work and leisure activities.

Parallel to these are certain developments in the therapist. He, too, begins to feel somewhat relaxed, finding himself freer from the countertransference pull toward taking or avoiding this or that stance. The therapist's experience is analogous to that of a mother during the later phases of separation-individuation.

> These feelings are twofold in nature. The parent feels a lessening of the demand for attention and libidinal gratification from the child who has successfully negotiated rapprochement; the analyst of the termination-ready patient feels a decrease in the transference demands. The analyst is less likely to be drawn into transference-countertransference enactments and feels less pressure to behave in ways foreign to himself. In addition to this direct response, the parent, by identification, senses the child's readiness to do more on his own; he can, for example, envision the child's spending the afternoon with a friend with the excitement that he himself feels about such activities rather than anxiety. Similarly, the analyst can picture the autonomous activities the patient describes with pleasure rather than with the feeling that this is a defensive retreat from the relationship. [Pulver 1991, pp. 402–403]

Yet another development is a dawning awareness of passing time on the part of both parties. The patient begins to mention various life goals (Ticho 1972) more frequently, and the therapist, too, becomes aware of their importance. Together, these changes in the subjective experience of the two partners, in the dynamics of the dyad, and in the overall ambience of the treatment setting, suggest that termination is at hand.

SUGGESTED READINGS

Giovacchini, P. L. (1972). Interpretation and definition of the analytic setting. In *Tactics and Technique in Psychoanalytic Therapy*, pp. 291–304. New York: Science House.

Pulver, S. E. (1991). Termination and separation-individuation. In *Beyond the Symbiotic Orbit: Advances in Separation-Individuation Theory — Essays in Honor of Selma Kramer, M.D.*, ed. S. Akhtar and H. Parens, pp. 389–404. Hillsdale, NJ: Analytic Press.

Ticho, E. (1972). Termination of psychoanalysis: treatment goals, life goals. *Psychoanalytic Quarterly* 41:315–333.

90. What are the steps in managing the termination phase?

A proper handling of termination is extremely important in the analytic treatment of individuals with severe character pathology. It should be done gradually and carefully, with the entire process being divided into *two subphases* (Rangell 1966). The first subphase extends from the day on which the therapist and the patient agree that the treatment might indeed be approaching its end to the day an actual ending date is decided upon. The second subphase extends from the setting of this date to the end of the last session. The duration of the first subphase is highly variable, depending upon the emergence of new feelings, regressive movements, and the interpretive resolution of both. The duration of the second subphase is more a matter of choice; four to six months (and sometimes even longer) seems a reasonable length of time to work through the deeper mourning process mobilized by the fixing of the actual termination date.

Many difficult and complex issues need to be tackled during the *first subphase*. The end of treatment for the patient means separating from a highly valued object, the therapist. Besides happiness and pride over his increasing psychic autonomy and over a job well done, the patient also experiences feelings of anxiety, rage, and sadness, the characteristic "termination triad" (Pulver 1991, p. 401). The patient might feel that the therapist is permitting the final separation because he, the patient, is not valued. The patient's self-esteem is hurt and he feels angry. This anger often mobilizes the "resolved" preoedipal and oedipal transferences of the aggressive type. Moreover, anxiety is experienced in regard to the patient's ability to sustain autonomous psychic welfare. This leads the patient to seek reassurances that he can return for "emotional refueling." The patient might give voice to a fear that once the treatment is over, he will never be allowed to return to the therapist for help. Such fears might emanate from continuing (or reemergent) superego constraints on dependent longings, but they might also contain a kernel of historical truth insofar as the patient might indeed have experienced a greater than ordinary withdrawal of parental (especially maternal) affection with each expectable, progressive step in development. At this time, therefore, the patient needs to be gently reminded of such relevant reconstructions made during the earlier periods of treatment. As anger and anxiety recede, the patient's desire for setting an actual termination date returns. A mutually convenient time, four to six months in the future, can now be agreed upon.

With the advent of the *second subphase*, increasing sadness begins to set in. Mourning is now clearly evident. Feelings of gratitude and "review dreams" that contain evidence of the structural changes made now appear. The patient becomes able to express happiness fearlessly about the prospect of being on his own. He utilizes his observing ego to a much greater extent in self-understanding. However, there is also an occasional revival of his symptoms and of a tendency to use "magical links" (Volkan 1987, p. 104) to hold on to the therapist. With interpretive amelioration of these issues, the actual end is at hand. Mourning continues after termination but the patient's ego is now capable of dealing with this on its own.

SUGGESTED READINGS

Pulver, S. E. (1991). Termination and separation-individuation. In *Beyond the Symbiotic Orbit: Advances in Separation-Individuation Theory — Essays in Honor of Selma Kramer, M.D.*, ed. S. Akhtar and H. Parens, pp. 389–404. Hillsdale, NJ: Analytic Press.

Rangell, L. (1966). An overview of the ending of an analysis. In *Psychoanalysis in the Americas*, ed. R. E. Litmin, pp. 141–173. New York: International Universities Press.

Volkan, V. D. (1987). *Six Steps in the Treatment of Borderline Personality Organization*. Northvale, NJ: Jason Aronson.

Part VI

PROGNOSIS AND
OUTCOME

91. How does aging affect the manifestations of severe personality disorders?

The diagnostic profiles of severe personality disorders refer to adult patients. However, adulthood is not static. *Adulthood repeatedly poses novel challenges, offers newer tasks to be mastered.* At first, it brings forth the need for consolidating of vocational identity and resolving conflicts and inhibitions regarding romance and marriage. Somewhat later, the intrapsychic and social dilemmas of parenthood appear on the horizon. Then, the onset of middle age introduces matters of time limits and a dawning awareness of one's mortality. There is a renewed recognition of personal myths, a deeper reworking of oedipal tasks (now also in their inverse form, i.e., vis-à-vis one's children), an acceptance of the limits of one's reach, a shift in time perspective, and, associated with all this, the beginning of a mourning process. This, nonetheless, has salutory effects upon the sense of one's true identity. Old age brings a new psychosocial context characterized by retirement, impending and real loss of loved ones, the potential envy of youth, physical deterioration, loneliness, and, in the midst of all this, the task of achieving wisdom and developing a post-ambivalent view of the world in which one has lived and which one is about to leave forever.

These challenges of unfolding adulthood often prove too difficult for individuals with already compromised ego-functions and splintered identities. Additional burdens come from changing social realities as well as alterations in the biological processes of the body. Together, these biopsychosocial stressors tax the ego (especially in severe personality disorders) and result in significant psychodynamic shifts. Newer symptoms emerge and relatively established behavior patterns recede into the background.

Narcissistic patients who were promiscuous in their youth, for instance, begin to settle down with the onset of middle age, whereas those who had remained restrained so far might, for the first time, begin a life of amorous adventures. Significant experiences of both success and disillusionment over the course of adult life tend to ameliorate the symptoms of pathological narcissism. An occasional crossover between the overt pictures of narcissistic and *schizoid personalities* has also been noted. *Borderline patients* tend to become anergic and less restless with advancing age. "Two bench marks of the disorder in younger patients do not appear to define the presentation of the disorder in late life. They are identity disturbance and the constellation of symptoms that include impulsivity, self-mutilation, risk-taking, and substance abuse" (Rosowsky and Gurian 1992, p. 387). *Antisocial individuals'* tendencies are also likely to burn out with age. Actually, a majority of individuals with both borderline and antisocial personality disorders no longer show the characteristic symptoms of the disorder by middle age. (Indeed, there is evidence of a high degree of recovery from borderline personality disorder after fifteen years; from about 50 to 75 percent of patients are then no longer diagnosable as borderline personalities.) Individuals with *paranoid personalities* usually fare better in old age than might be expected. Their fighting stance keeps them intact; failure is never their own. The world at large has to be taken on in single combat; life presents a diverting struggle against dangerous external forces and there is little time for despair.

All this suggests a greater phenotypal flexibility in the syndromes of severe character pathology than has hitherto been suspected.

SUGGESTED READINGS

Paris, J. (1993). The treatment of borderline personality disorder in light of the research on its long term outcome. *Canadian Journal of Psychiatry* 38: (Suppl. 1)28–34.

Rosowsky, E., and Gurian, B. (1992). Impact of borderline personality disorder in late life on systems of care. *Hospital and Community Psychiatry* 43:386–389.

Stone, M. H. (1990). *The Fate of Borderline Patients: Successful Outcome and Psychiatric Practice.* New York: Guilford.

92. Do specific types of severe personality disorders have different outcomes?

The long-term prognosis of severe personality disorders does seem to vary with specific diagnostic categories (e.g., narcissistic, borderline, antisocial). However, *variables other than descriptive diagnosis (e.g., vocational adjustment, social supports, alcohol and drug abuse) carry a much greater weight vis-à-vis long-term outcome.* Therefore, even within a specific diagnostic subgroup the outcome of individual patients differs (at times dramatically), owing to the uneven distribution of the ego, superego, and extraneous factors affecting the prognosis. For instance, borderline patients who possess an inherent talent (musical, artistic, or literary), high intelligence, "charm," and self discipline have better long-term outcomes than those borderline patients without such gifts. Conversely, borderline patients with a history of severe childhood sexual abuse have lesser chances of recovery than those borderlines who either had less severe childhood sexual abuse or no sexual abuse (Paris et al. 1993). Similarly, narcissistic patients with a greater sense of morality and internalized value systems have a better prognosis than those narcissistic patients who display antisocial tendencies. And, narcissistic patients with extreme exploitativeness and lack of empathy have a poorer prognosis than those narcissistic patients without these features.

With such reservations in mind, it can be said that some diagnostic constellations are associated with a good and others with a bad prognosis (Kernberg 1975). In the former group are histrionic (infantile) personalities, narcissistic personalities with no overt manifestations of ego-weakness, and those borderline personalities who possess honesty, talent, psychological mindedness, and capacity for perseverance. In the latter group, most prominent are the individuals with antisocial personality disorder. Hypomanic personalities, characteristically averse to the contemplative sadness mobilized by intensive psychotherapy, also have a poor prognosis. Narcissistic personalities with signs of generalized ego-weakness (e.g., poor frustration tolerance, impaired sublimatory capacity, and lack of impulse control) have a guarded prognosis. Paranoid and schizoid patients also have a poor prognosis. As far as individuals with sexual perversions are concerned, those with fixed single perversions and severe narcissistic personalities seem to have a worse prognosis than clearly borderline patients with multiple perverse fantasies and actions in the context of unstable object relations.

It is interesting to note that *many of Kernberg's ideas, stated nearly two decades ago, have found support in recent empirical research*. Michael Stone (1990), in a long-term follow-up study of individuals with severe personality disorders, found that paranoid, schizoid, and schizotypal traits do have a negative effect on outcome. Prognosis is even worse when the patient meets the diagnostic criteria for both borderline and antisocial personality disorders. The "impulsive, hostile, rageful, and self-injurious traits" (p. 91) of such patients render them even more prone to a poor outcome than is the case for antisocial personalities without borderline features. Another group that had an "abysmal outcome" (p. 99) was constituted by those in whom narcissistic, antisocial, and paranoid features coexisted; this is the triad subsumed under the rubric of "malignant narcissism" by Kernberg.

SUGGESTED READINGS

Kernberg, O. F. (1975). *Borderline Conditions and Pathological Narcissism*, pp. 111–152. New York: Jason Aronson.

Paris, J., Zweig-Frank, H., and Guzder, H. (1993). The role of psychological risk factors in recovery from borderline personality disorder. *Comprehensive Psychiatry* 34:410–413.

Stone, M. H. (1990). *The Fate of Borderline Patients: Successful Outcome and Psychiatric Practice*. New York: Guilford.

93. Are there gender-related differences in prognosis and outcome?

Yes. Male and female patients with severe personality disorders to tend to have somewhat different long-term outcomes. However three caveats must be kept in mind here: (1) Differences in symptomatology of severe personality disorders in both sexes might exist from the very beginning and these differences might affect prognosis and outcome; (2) There exists a number of prognostic variables that are limited to women by definition. These include premenstrual dysphoria, pregnancy, children born out of wedlock, and so on; (3) Finally, there might be stressful events (e.g., rape) or co-morbid syndromes (e.g., bulimia, anorexia nervosa) that occur primarily in women and thus alter the outcome of their personality disorders. Together, these three factors contribute to the differences in the prognosis of severe personality disorders in the two sexes.

Gender-related differences in outcome were amply evident, for instance, in the follow-up study of residentially treated borderline patients by Bardenstein and McGlashan (1988). Female patients in their sample were more likely to have already been married, to be suffering from depressive symptomatology, and to be giving a history of clear-cut precipitating factors. Male patients, on the other hand, had more trouble with the law. The patients were followed up from two to thirty-two years and revealed a more or less consistent life trajectory. Their lives displayed much disorganization during their 20s and into their early 30s, followed by improvement during their 40s. Some patients showed worsening in their 50s mostly as a consequence of the dissolution (through divorce or death, for instance) of a close relationship. Overall, women seemed to do worse than men in this sample. They became increasingly depressed upon entering their 40s and this destabilized their much needed relationships. Men, on the other hand, improved in their work performance and seemed to depend less on emotional support from romantic and sexual partners.

A more recent long-term follow-up study of borderline patients by Stone (1990) also showed gender-related differences in outcome. These were, however, not the same as found in the Bardenstein and McGlashan study. In Stone's experience, female borderline patients (with or without a major affective disorder) appeared to have significantly better outcomes than male borderline patients. The proportion of those who turned to alcohol was not significantly different in the two sexes, although the suicide rate was higher among female borderline patients with concomitant alcoholism and a major affective disorder. The presence of eating disorders, more common in female borderline patients, also tended to render the prognosis poor. Interestingly, physical beauty and attractiveness among female borderline patients contributed to a more favorable outcome. Most such patients were doing better on follow-up, with many being quite successful. Stone eloquently describes the situation. It is as if these women

possess, like the cat, . . . a righting mechanism permitting them to land always on their feet. Many had led checkered existences before coming to the hospital and for varying lengths of time afterward, reeling from one crisis (romantic breakup, suicide gesture, etc.) to another. But another potential rescuer was always at hand ready to take up where a previous protector had left off. Or else a previous protector was willing to contemplate reconciliation after an outburst of hostility on the part of a borderline woman that would have led to a permanent rift had she been less attractive. [Stone 1990, p. 148]

SUGGESTED READINGS

Akhtar, S. (1992). *Broken Structures: Severe Personality Disorders and Their Treatment*, pp. 270–271. Northvale, NJ: Jason Aronson.

Bardenstein, K. K., and McGlashan, T. H. (1988). The natural history of a residentially treated borderline sample: gender differences. *Journal of Personality Disorders* 2:69–83.

Stone, M. H. (1990). *The Fate of Borderline Patients: Successful Outcome and Psychiatric Practice*, pp. 137–158. New York: Guilford.

94. What factors govern the long-term prognosis of narcissistic personality disorder?

In 1975, Kernberg outlined the following nine prognostic indicators for narcissistic personality disorder: (1)*Tolerance of sadness*: Chances for a favorable outcome are better for those narcissistic patients who possess some capacity for mournful sadness, especially when accompanied by feelings of guilt and concern towards others. (2) *Secondary gain of being in analysis*: When individuals with narcissistic personalities derive social advantages from being in analysis, their prognosis suffers. On the surface, such gains (e.g., analytic treatment as a part of getting qualified as an analyst) are professional but on a deeper level they express an unconscious wish to steal the analyst's skills, to deny envy of him, and to circumvent genuine dependency upon him. (3) *Transference potential for guilt versus paranoia*: Narcissistic patients invariably avoid attachment and dependency upon the analyst. However, the degree to which such avoidance is based on unconscious guilt (as against upon paranoid tendencies) determines the prognosis; the more it is guilt-based, the better the outcome. (4) *Sublimatory potential*: Narcissistic patients often have interests in art, music, and literature. Moreover, they are often quite successful in their particular fields of work. However, it is not merely the external measures of their success but the actual quality and depth of their interests that determines the prognosis. (5) *Superego integration*: While most narcissistic patients display subtle superego defects, some may indeed be quite "honest in money matters, in keeping promises, and in emotionally uninvolved daily interactions with others" (Kernberg 1975, p. 253). These patients have a better prognosis than those who are thoroughly corrupt. (6) *Narcissistic supplies from external reality*: Narcissistic individuals in positions of power might surround themselves with sycophants, admirers, and "yes men" and thus maintain their grandiose selves intact. Such chronic enactment works against the analytic process and reduces its potential benefit. (7) *Impulse control and anxiety tolerance*: Prognosis is better for patients with greater impulse control and anxiety tolerance than for those with weaker capacities in this area, especially if combined with substance abuse. (8) *Regressive potential*: Prognosis is guarded for patients who tend to readily regress to primary process. and (9) *Motivation for treatment*: The more the individual truly wishes to overcome his inner coldness, feelings of emptiness, and incapacity to empathize with others, the better the prognosis. On the other hand, the more the narcissistic individual seeks to become truly "perfect" by undergoing analysis, the more guarded is the prognosis.

Recent follow-up studies have upheld many of these findings, although their patient samples are not comprised of individuals who have undergone psychoanalysis. Stone (1989), reporting on a sample of hospitalized patients, found that the admixture of narcissistic and antisocial features and extreme lack of empathy were frequently associated with a poor outcome. On the other hand, artistic talent, high intelligence, attractiveness, and self-discipline were associated with a favorable outcome. The only prospective follow-up study of carefully diagnosed narcissistic patients (Ronningstam et al. in press) reveals that a significant reduction in pathological narcissism over a period of time is associated with actual success (which diminishes the need for grandiose elaboration), new, durable relationships (which satisfy the need for being mirrored), and even some experiences of disillusionment (which enhance the acceptance of realistic limits).

SUGGESTED READINGS

Kernberg, O. F. (1975). *Borderline Conditions and Pathological Narcissism*, pp. 248–257. New York: Jason Aronson.

Ronnigstam E., Gunderson, J., and Lyons, M. (in press). Changes in pathological narcissism. *American Journal of Psychiatry*.

Stone, M. H. (1989). Long term follow-up of narcissistic/borderline patients. *Psychiatric Clinics of North America* 12:621–641.

95. How does a history of incest affect the phenomenology, prognosis, and outcome of severe personality disorders?

Incest is invariably harmful to its victim. While an individual with such trauma might develop a certain self-reliance, ambition, perseverance, and tenacious pursuit of self-knowledge, the fact remains that incest is inimical to normal, healthy development. It results in lifelong mistrust of others, chronic guilt, sadomasochistic tendencies, inhibited or counterphobically exaggerated sexuality, a vague but persistent feeling of impending disaster, and vulnerability to psychosomatic phenomena, accidents, injuries, and even suicide. However, *since incest usually occurs in the setting of multiple traumas (e.g., emotional deprivation, physical abuse, parental alcoholism), it is difficult to isolate its uniquely pathogenic effects.*

Such caveats aside, empirical observation does suggest an association between a history of incest and the diagnosis of borderline personality disorder. Estimates of its occurrence among female borderline patients reach as high as 50 percent (Stone 1990); male borderline patients less frequently give histories of such victimization. In a study of 1,040 consecutively hospitalized psychiatric patients (Brown and Anderson 1991), the diagnosis of borderline personality disorder was found to be much more frequent among the abused victims than the non-abused patients. A significant step-wise increase in the proportion of patients with borderline personality disorder was observed with increasing levels of reported abuse: 3 percent of non-abused patients, 13 percent of patients who had been either sexually or physically abused, and 29 percent of those with both types of abuse. Moreover, in light of "the frequent difficulties such patients have with trust, it can be hypothesized that many of the patients with borderline personality disorder in the 'non-abused group' had actually been abused but they had either dissociated

these experiences or chosen not to discuss them with their therapists" (Brown and Anderson 1991, p. 59). The correlation between
incest and the adult borderline condition, especially in women
with a clearly diagnosable borderline personality disorder, might
therefore be even stronger than suggested by the preceding
numbers. Indeed, many of the clinical features of borderline
personality (e.g., chronic cynicism and anger, sexual dysregula-
tion, feelings of inferiority, self-mutilation, and suicidal tendencies) can be related to the prior incest experience. The most
impressive piece of evidence for a relatively specific pathogenic
role of incest in borderline pathology is that whereas both
borderline and schizophrenic patients come from chaotic families,
only the former have frequently been victims of incest as children
(Stone 1990).

*Not only does the incest experience seem to play a role in the
pathogenesis of the borderline condition, it also alters the long-
term course and outcome of the disorder.* In Stone's (1990) study
of borderline patients, there was "a tendency for the incest victims
to remain more impaired at follow-up (10–23 years later)" (p. 122).
Not surprisingly, those borderline patients who had a combined
trauma history—parental brutality and incest—did significantly
worse than those only sexually abused. Based upon this finding,
Stone suggests that "[p]erhaps the effects of abuse are particularly
noxious where the emotional background is one of parental
hatred, rather than of (exploitative) love—as is present in some
cases of abuse and in many cases of incest. Children can forgive
inappropriate love more easily than withering rejection" (p. 134).

SUGGESTED READINGS

Brown, G. R., and Anderson, B. (1991). Psychiatric morbidity in adult in-
    patients with childhood histories of sexual and physical abuse. *American
    Journal of Psychiatry* 148:55–61.
Stone, M. H. (1990). *The Fate of Borderline Patients: Successful Outcome and
    Psychiatric Practice*, pp. 116–136. New York: Guilford.
_____ (1992). Incest, Freud's seduction theory, and borderline personality.
    Journal of the American Academy of Psychoanalysis 20:167–181.

96. What factors govern the drop-out rates in the psychotherapy of borderline patients?

Borderline patients often drop out of psychotherapy prematurely. This is not surprising. Meaningful psychotherapy always poses requirements for the patient. These include patience, collaboration, discipline in keeping regular appointments, willingness to look at one's own attitudes and behaviors, and, above all, a capacity to tolerate the ambivalence inevitable in a sustained relationship. Borderline patients have impairments in these capacities and are therefore vulnerable to interrupt the psychotherapeutic undertaking. Estimates of their drop-out rate range from a low of 16 percent (Linehan, quoted in Yeomans et al. 1992, p. 186) to a high of 67 percent (Skodol et al. 1983).

Frank Yeomans and colleagues (1992) have recently reported on their experience with a "contract-based approach" to psychodynamic psychotherapy of borderline patients. The drop-out rate among their patients was 35 percent. Yeomans and colleagues attempted to discern the factors governing the proclivity to drop out of treatment. According to their observations, the mere severity of borderline symptomatology does not forecast a high drop-out rate. However, borderline patients with sustained higher level of daily functioning do tend to stay longer in treatment. Honesty, candor, and willingness to share conflicted feelings with the therapist were also associated with a longer stay in treatment. The time in the patient's life or in the course of the disorder at which treatment is undertaken is also significant. Patients "who have failed in previous treatment contracts, and who 'hit bottom,' are those most likely to engage in treatment" (Yeomans et al. 1992, p. 193). Moving on to the therapist variables, Yeomans and colleagues found that experienced therapists have lower drop-out rates than inexperienced therapists. Moreover, when patients of experienced therapists drop out, they do so later in the course of treatment than the patients of inexperienced therapists. The clear setting of an initial contract and the development (and maintenance) of a therapeutic alliance correlated positively with a lower drop-out rate. Another important finding was that the patients who did not discuss terminating treatment were often the ones who ended up dropping out prematurely. Those who talked about it openly were less likely to act upon such an inclination. This suggests that therapists should scan the patient's associations for clues to intentions of dropping out and should bring these up for mutual discussion.

A word of caution is warranted. The drop-outs reported by Yeomans and his colleagues occurred by the third month of psychotherapy. Such ruptures of treatment often herald an unfavorable long-term outcome for the patient. In contrast are those patients who also stop treatment against the therapist's advice, but only after having being engaged in psychotherapy for a considerably long period. Such dropping out might still be compatible with a reasonably successful therapeutic result (Waldinger and Gunderson 1984). Indeed, patients who are very ego-impaired and whose treatments are characterized by profound sadomasochistic enactments, often end the treatment as they achieve object constancy and as oedipal transferences begin to emerge. Their treatment appears to them now as having diminishing returns and their burgeoning ego capacities are sufficient reward to consider termination. To regard this decision as dropping out is not infrequently reflective of the therapist's difficulty in letting go of the patient and his unrealistic goals from the treatment.

SUGGESTED READINGS

Skodol, A., Buckley, P., and Charles, E. (1983). Is there a characteristic pattern to the treatment history of clinic outpatients with borderline personality? *Journal of Nervous and Mental Disease* 171: 405–410.

Waldinger, R., and Gunderson, J. (1984). Completed psychotherapies with borderline patients. *American Journal of Psychotherapy* 38:190–202.

Yeomans, F. E., Selzer, M. A., and Clarkin, J. F. (1992). *Treating the Borderline Patient: A Contract-Based Approach.* New York: Basic Books.

97. How often do borderline patients commit suicide and can those at high risk be identified early on?

First and foremost, it should be noted that contrary to the stereotype, *borderline patients are not the ones with the highest incidence of completed suicide among various psychiatric patients*. Actually, their suicide rate is not significantly different from that of schizophrenics or people with bipolar disorder. (The highest suicide rate is associated with the diagnosis of schizoaffective disorder.) At the same time, the fact is that some borderline patients do end up killing themselves. The estimates of the proportion of borderline patients who do so range from 8 to 12 percent.

In an impressive follow-up study with an average post discharge interval of 16 ½ years, Stone (1990) was able to trace 192 of the original 206 hospitalized borderline patients. Of these, 17 (8.9 percent) had committed suicide. Based on a careful analysis of the clinical and demographic characteristics of this sample, Stone arrived at the following conclusions:

(1) Suicide risk is particularly high in males with borderline personality disorder and a concomitant major affective disorder. In general, however, male borderline patients are not at a greater risk than females.

(2) The group at highest risk is composed of females with *DSM-III* type borderline personality disorder, concomitant major affective disorder, and alcohol abuse. When all three features were present in women, the suicide rate jumped to 38 percent.

(3) Factors usually associated with increased risk of suicide (e.g., being single, living alone, being unemployed, lack of social supports, alcohol or drug abuse, acute life crises including the loss of a therapist) figure prominently in the background of those borderlines who commit suicide.

(4) Unlike an earlier study (Kullgren 1988), which had found

a tendency toward higher completed suicides in borderline patients with multiple as opposed to single previous attempts, Stone's study did not find this to be true.

(5) Distinguishing serious suicidal attempts from suicidal gestures is not always easy and a history of the latter frequently exists in the background of even those borderline patients who end up actually committing suicide.

(6) The occurrence of suicidal attempts and even gestures is more worrisome in male than in female patients with borderline personality disorder.

(7) Those who commit suicide choose violent methods (e.g., shooting, jumping off buildings) more often than overdoses. This tendency was more apparent in males.

(8) Finally, those borderline patients who attempted suicide, came very close to dying, and were miraculously saved at the last minute were profoundly affected by their near-death experience. Almost all such patients in Stone's study sooner or later gave up suicidal ideation altogether and some even found a renewed dedication to leading a meaningful life.

From all this, it is quite clear that some borderline patients do commit suicide and that this risk is much greater in those who (1) meet the *DSM-III* or *DSM-III-R* criteria for borderline personality disorder, (2) have a concomitant major affective disorder, (3) lack social supports, (4) drink excessively, and (5) are faced with a sudden life change. Since seemingly manipulative suicidal gestures are not infrequent among even those borderline individuals who do end up killing themselves, there is every reason to take such gestures with the utmost seriousness, more so if the individual matches the profile outlined above.

SUGGESTED READINGS

Kullgren, G. (1988). Factors associated with completed suicide in borderline personality disorder. *Journal of Nervous and Mental Disease* 176:40–44.

Paris, J., Brown, R., and Nowlis, D. (1987). Long term follow-up of borderline patients. *Comprehensive Psychiatry* 28:530–535.

Stone, M. H. (1990). *The Fate of Borderline Patients: Successful Outcome and Psychiatric Practice*, pp. 40–65. New York: Guilford.

98. Are there patients who require lifelong treatment?

Many, if not most, practicing analysts and psychotherapists end up having one or two patients who require lifelong help. This group of patients is comprised of three types of individuals.

(1) *The first group* is made up of patients who have a severely traumatic background, strong genetic predisposition to affective or cognitive instability, and a checkered history of pathologic and unstable relationships. They have tried diverse treatments including psychotherapy, medications, psychoanalysis (especially if they come from affluent families), and, at times, even some esoteric methods. Nothing seems to help them. They continue to suffer from chronic dysphoria, uncertainty, feelings of inferiority, a vaguely depressive pain, a gnawing sense of being alienated from others, hypochondria, and a barely controlled dread of psychic breakdown. They keep seeking psychotherapeutic help, though perhaps with diminishing frequency, even as they grow old.

(2) *The second group* comes from the analyst's or psychotherapist's own practice. It is composed of individuals with whom the therapist has, over a long period of time, gradually slipped out of a technically neutral position. Frequently, such patients are extremely socially isolated and the analyst is their sole meaningful object. Under such circumstances, transference analysis, especially in the realm of aggression, is very difficult (perhaps impossible). The ego weakness of such patients further pressures the therapist to "take over," with the concomitant erosion of neutrality resulting in "appropriate" advice giving and other no less rationalized "supportive" interventions. The result is a state of near-addiction to the therapist.

(3) *The third group* is composed of individuals who suffer from a "pathological hope" (Amati-Mehler and Argentieri 1989, p. 300) that psychotherapy or psychoanalysis can actually reverse or wipe out certain devastating traumas or losses in their developmental background.

In such cases the psychoanalyst may collude for years with the patients' need to be psychoneurotic (as opposed to mad) and to be treated as psychoneurotic. The analysis goes well, and everyone is pleased. The only drawback is that the analysis never ends. It can be terminated, and the patient may even mobilize a psychoneurotic false self for the purpose of finishing and expressing gratitude. But, in fact, the patient knows that there has been no change in the underlying (psychotic) state and the analyst and the patient have succeeded in colluding to bring about a failure. [Winnicott 1971, p. 102]

While these three types of patients inadvertently end up becoming what is sometimes derogatorily called "lifers," I suggest that *lifelong intervention should be an actively chosen treatment strategy for some patients*. Certain grossly ego-impaired and yet marginally socially adapted, geographically remote, reclusive, and unmotivated patients should be seen "on demand" (Winnicott 1971) for a few sessions during crisis situations only, every few months, or perhaps even every few years. No sustained treatment should be attempted. Instead, the psychotherapist should tell them that he would be willing to see them within 24–48 hours of their call for a few sessions off and on throughout their life. The reassuring though "silent" availability of the therapist during intervals between these brief interventions is itself their ongoing treatment.

SUGGESTED READINGS

Akhtar, S. (1992). *Broken Structures: Severe Personality Disorders and Their Treatment*, pp. 306–307. Northvale, NJ: Jason Aronson.

Amati-Mehler, J., and Argentieri, S. (1989). Hope and hopelessness: a technical problem? *International Journal of Psycho-Analysis* 70:295–304.

Winnicott, D. W. (1971). *Playing and Reality*. London: Penguin.

99. What factors indicate an unfavorable prognosis for severe personality disorders?

In 1975, Kernberg reported on the prognostic variables in border-line conditions derived from his analysis of the clinical data of the Psychotherapy Research Project of The Menninger Foundation. Essentially, he found three areas suggesting a poor outcome:

(1) *Specific diagnostic categories*: Antisocial personality disorder has the worst prognosis among the various types of severe personality disorders. Hypomanic personalities also have a poor prognosis because they are often not engageable in psychotherapy. Narcissistic personalities with overt borderline functioning, that is, with signs of generalized ego-weakness, also carry a poor prognosis. Paranoid and schizoid personalities have a guarded prognosis. In the case of paranoid patients, especially those functioning on an overt borderline level, the prognosis improves if the treatment can be structured so that their need for omnipotent control does not seriously handicap the therapeutic relationship. In the case of schizoid patients, the tendency toward an unrelenting withdrawal from the therapeutic interaction drains the patient–therapist relationship of all meaning, even a basic human element. In such circumstances, therefore, the natural warmth and genuine responsiveness of the therapist becomes a crucial variable in determining prognosis.

(2) *Specific symptomatic constellations*: Borderline patients without neurotic symptoms (e.g., anxiety, depression, phobic inhibitions) have a poorer prognosis than those borderline patients who do display such symptoms. Severe and chronic social isolation coupled with a sexual life restricted to masturbation with perverse fantasies, also heralds an unfavorable outcome. Poor prognosis is also associated with ego-syntonicity of maladaptive character traits, impaired capacity for genuine remorse, and a tendency to have self-destruction as an idealized life goal. The presence of alcoholism and substance abuse also renders the

prognosis poor, especially if underlying these symptoms is a narcissistic personality structure.

(3) *Specific treatment variables*: Unfavorable outcome is also associated with certain treatment variables including: (a) poor "fit" between the therapist and patient, (b) deficient capacity on the therapist's part to integrate his countertransference reactions into the technique of psychotherapy, and (c) certain specific characterologic problems in the therapist, especially unresolved narcissism, weak object constancy, and difficulty with aggression.

It is interesting to note that many of these predictors of negative outcome, outlined nearly thirty years ago, have been upheld in recent empirical research. Stone (1990), for instance, in a follow-up study of hospitalized borderline patients with an average post-discharge period of 16½ years, confirmed the validity of many of the ideas expressed above. He found a poor outcome to be consistently associated with chronic irritability, explosiveness, paranoid and schizoid tendencies, "malignant narcissism," and antisocial proclivities. At the same time, not all antisocial patients did poorly on follow-up. By their 30s and 40s, many had "mellowed without further treatment into trustworthy, respectable members of their community" (pp. 86–87). Stone emphasized that negative attributes seldom mentioned in discussions of personality—tactlessness, rigidity, and pettiness, for instance—at times affect the outcome more adversely than the usually recognized symptom clusters and/or descriptive diagnostic categories.

SUGGESTED READINGS

Kernberg, O. F. (1975). *Borderline Conditions and Pathological Narcissism*, pp. 111–152. New York: Jason Aronson.

Kernberg, O. F., Burstein, E., Coyne, L., et al. (1972). Psychotherapy and psychoanalysis: final report of The Menninger Foundation's Psychotherapy Research Project, *Bulletin of the Menninger Clinic* 36:1–85.

Stone, M. H. (1990). *The Fate of Borderline Patients: Successful Outcome and Psychiatric Practice*. New York: Guilford.

100. What factors indicate a favorable prognosis for severe personality disorders?

In 1975, Kernberg reported on prognostic variables in severe personality disorders derived from his analysis of the clinical data of the Psychotherapy Research Project of The Menninger Foundation. He found three areas indicating a favorable outcome. (1) *Specific diagnostic categories*: Hysterical personalities functioning on an overt borderline level and infantile (histrionic, in current terminology) personalities usually have a good prognosis with psychoanalytic psychotherapy. Narcissistic personalities with relatively intact ego-functioning, too, if treated with psychoanalysis, have a good prognosis. (2) *Specific symptomatic constellations*: Besides the absence of clinical features associated with a poor outcome (e.g., substance abuse, antisocial trends, malignant narcissism), there are some features that suggest a favorable prognosis. These include presence of anxiety, high sublimatory potential, good superego functioning, and at least some stability of object relations. Anxiety is a good predictor for improvement because it provides a motivating force to seek and sustain treatment. Sublimatory potential, revealed in "the extent to which a patient is able to invest himself in a certain activity or profession beyond strictly narcissistic needs, the degree of gratification from such activity or profession, and the extent to which the patient is concerned about the intrinsic values of the activity or profession" (Kernberg 1975, p. 133), also improves the prognosis of severe personality disorders. The same is true of a good superego. "The more awareness borderline patients have of values other than their own satisfactions, the more of an abstracted, depersonified superego structure is presumably present and the better the prognosis" (p. 138). In the realm of object relations too, the greater the capacity to tolerate simultaneously loving and hateful feelings toward the same person (i.e., the less readily the ego resorts to splitting), the better the prognosis. (3) *Specific treatment vari-*

ables: While acknowledging that it is difficult to separate the influence of the therapist's personality from that of his technique, Kernberg agreed with the report of The Menninger Foundation Research Project, which had concluded that the therapist's "capacity to integrate creatively his personality traits and countertransference reactions into the technique, is the most crucial factor in the outcome of the treatment of patients with a low level of psychic functioning, that is, ego weakness" (p. 147). Kernberg also voiced agreement with Guntrip that the therapist's personality becomes especially crucial in the treatment of severely schizoid patients.

More recent follow-up studies (McGlashan 1985, Stone 1992) have largely upheld these findings while adding some of their own. Stone (1990), for instance, found that absence of substance abuse and marked antisocial trends, and the presence of honesty and sustained relationships heralded a better prognosis. Stone also observed certain positive "soft signs" whose long-term effect often outweighed the more easily recognized negative "hard signs." "Likableness (and the absence of marked hostility or mendacity), candor, perseverance, talent, attractiveness, and the like may win out eventually over traumatic factors (if they are not too severe), florid symptoms at the height of illness, and so on" (Stone 1990, p. 284). These attributes enhance the likelihood of forming an alliance with a therapist and sustaining relationships with friends and lovers. Is it then a surprise that these attributes improve the chances of a favorable outcome?

SUGGESTED READINGS

Kernberg, O. F. (1975). *Borderline Conditions and Pathological Narcissism*, pp. 111–152. New York: Jason Aronson

McGlashan, T. H. (1985). The prediction of outcome in borderline personality disorder: Part V of the Chestnut Lodge follow-up study. In *The Borderline: Current Empirical Research*, pp. 63–98. Washington, DC: American Psychiatric Press.

Stone, M. H. (1990). *The Fate of Borderline Patients: Successful Outcome and Psychiatric Practice*. New York: Guilford.

Index

About the Author

Salman Akhtar, M.D., F.A.P.A. is Professor of Psychiatry at Jefferson Medical College in Philadelphia and a training and supervising analyst at the Philadelphia Psychoanalytic Institute. Dr. Akhtar is a member of the Group for Advancement of Psychiatry, the American College of Psychiatrists, and the Board of Directors of the Margaret S. Mahler Psychiatric Research Foundation. He serves on the editorial boards of *The International Journal of Psycho-Analysis, Mind and Human Interaction,* and *Psychiatry Today* and reviews papers for seven additional journals. In the recent past, he has served on the editorial board of the *Journal of the American Psychoanalytic Association*, and the Committee on Scientific Activities of the American Psychoanalytic Association. His more than 90 scientific publications include the book *Broken Structures: Severe Personality Disorders and Their Treatment* (1992) and six edited or co-edited books: *New Psychiatric Syndromes:* DSM-III *and Beyond* (1983), *The Trauma of Transgression: Psychotherapy of Incest Victims* (1991), *Beyond the Symbiotic Orbit: Advances in Separation- Individuation Theory—Essays in Honor of Selma Kramer, M.D.* (1992), *When the Body Speaks: Psychological Meanings in Kinetic Clues* (1992), *Mahler and Kohut: Perspectives on Development, Psychopathology and Technique* (1994), and *The Birth of Hatred: Clinical, Development, and Technical Aspects of Intense Aggression* (1995). Dr. Akhtar has been the recipient of the Jefferson Medical College's Robert Waelder Memorial Award for excellence in psychiatric teaching and has also published four volumes of poetry.